Welsh Poetry Competition

The First Five Years

An anthology of the winning
entries from 2007-2011

Editor
Dave Lewis

Ponty Press

Published by Ponty Press 2011

Special thanks to John Evans, Mike Jenkins, Sally Spedding
and all those who've entered and supported the competition
in our first five years

ISBN: 978-1-4477-3232-7

Front cover photograph & design: Dave Lewis

Websites:
www.welshpoetry.co.uk
www.david-lewis.co.uk

"An intellectual says a simple thing in a hard way.
An artist says a hard thing in a simple way."
— *Charles Bukowski*

CONTENTS

Introduction   1

The 2007 Winners   5

Concrete by Gavin Price   7

My body is old porridge by Eloise Williams   9

space by Amanda Weeks   11

Judges' comments   12

Specially Commended, 2007   15

Her hairs not short by Gavin Price   17

Solar Plexus by Jane Fox   19

Flights of Fancy by Richard Garman   21

In 1968... by John Gallas   22

Balancing Mixed Vegetables On A Motorway Bridge
by Clive Gilson   23

Fragments of Cardiff by Kate Scarratt   24

On Eric Gill - typophile etc. by Emily Hinshelwood   26

To Orpheus@lyre.com by Kate Noakes   28

Urban Tales by Phil Knight   29

Swansea Bay Promenade by Isobel Norris   30

Bags by Roger Barnett   31

What I am by Carrie-Ann Fry   32

Inside Out by Anthony Keating 33

Connecting by Leah Armstead 34

Extinction by Cerys Jones 35

The Size Zero Debate by Emma Sullivan 36

Bus Ride by Josiah Rowlands 37

The 2008 Winners 39

Visually-speaking by Emily Hinshelwood 41

Polyfiller by Clare Ferguson-Walker 43

I don't do hugs by Eloise Williams 45

Judges' comments 47

Specially Commended, 2008 51

On deck with Alun Lewis, the secret sleeper
by Owen Lowery 53

Trout by James Gower 55

Forget-Me-Not by Leah Ebdon 56

Hide by Jane Galletly 57

Learning from Buzzards by Roger Elkin 58

Watching Layers Form by Jenny Adamthwaite 60

Pen-y-Fan Revisited by Christopher Rogers 61

Barry Island revisited by Emyr Jones 63

Boireann by Graham Burchell 64

Show me the money by Amanda Weeks 66

Union Cat by Patricia Bellotti   68

Flies on Coke by Ellie Madden   69

on Davaar Island by John Gallas   71

Mad Mike: he's a motorbike manual
                                                                 73
by (Merv Read)/Read the Rock-Poet

Tower by John Watkins   75

Birthday Lunch by Pip Smith   76

His greatest fear by Leah Armstead   78

The Milky Way by Megan Vaughan   79

The 2009 Winners   81

the origami lesson by John Gallas   83

Nan Follows the Bikers on a Day Out by Eluned Rees   85

Rails by Lynn Roberts   87

Judges' comments   88

Specially Commended, 2009   91

Shipbuilding by David Ford   93

Corposant by Gareth Roberts   95

Wasted by Gareth Roberts   97

When she was very young by Rebecca Carrington   98

Wasp... by David Butler   99

Luna by Ben Ziman-Bright   101

Pins by Graham Burchell   102

Buzzards over Fleam Dyke by Harry Goode 104

One more to work the Oliver Hammer 1899
by Silvia Millward 105

A walk with God by Patricia Bellotti 107

Easter Monday by Isobel Norris 108

The Gatekeeper by Deborah Harvey 109

First Baron Cawdor of Castlemartin
by Emily Hinshelwood 110

Finding the Darkness by James Knox Whittet 111

lights in water by John Gallas 113

Head Case by Phil Knight 114

The day I ate what I thought was a magic mushroom
by Leah Armstead 116

The 2010 Winners 119

Litzmannstadt 1941 by Sally Spedding 121

Izzy by Nigel Ormond 123

Waiting by Jane Fox 125

Judges' comments 127

Specially Commended, 2010 131

Jetsam by Noel Williams 133

Polly by Ashley Bovan 134

A pen portrait of my ex-lover by Penny James 135

Shifts by Pat Borthwick 137

Still by Sue Lovell 138

Mr Selvridge Sketches by Richard Halperin 140

Llandudno by Helen Johnson 142

When you know the party's over... by J.S. Watts 143

Cynical Saviour? (maybe) by John Lusardi 144

Different by Jo Walters 146

Going Back by Terry Jones 147

the 2154 of this land by Steve Garside 149

A weekend at the coast by Meghan Tally 150

Estuary by Gareth Roberts 151

"you only like the idea of me..." by Alisa Lockwood 153

Rock, Scissors, Paper by Clare Scott 155

Carmarthen by Jeno Davies 156

The 2011 Winners 157

Horseshoe Bat by David J Costello 159

The Carpenter's Daughter by Kathy Miles 160

Night's Spy-glass by Moira Andrew 162

Judges' comments 163

Specially Commended, 2011 165

Stitches by Fatima Al Matar 167

Ah, you should see the mighty Deere by Mary Ryan 168

In Bloom by Tom Gatehouse 169

Perce Blackborow by Glyn Edwards 172

Lightwells by Alana Kelsall 174

Kasaks of Mongolia by Mary Irvine 178

Belted Gaberdines by Joy Winkler 179

Aim by Louise Wilford 180

Seal Clubbing by Glyn Edwards 182

Girl on the Underground by Alisa Lockwood 183

Bridgend by Mark Lock 184

Silas Jones by Anthony Fisher 186

Ode to Joy by Emily Hinshelwood 187

Beacon and Elks by Sheila Barksdale 188

Mackworth Street by Jenny Powell 190

The Painter's Holiday by Jenny Powell 191

Don't call your father a bastard by Ceri Rees 192

Index of titles 193

Introduction

This first *Welsh Poetry Competition* anthology is a collection of over 100 poems that our three esteemed judges considered worthy of a prize in the first five years of the competition, from our launch on 1st March 2007 to the announcement of results on 15th July 2011.

This compilation is not for the faint hearted, nor for those only interested in establishment praise or recognition. This book is purely for those who care passionately about one of the greatest art forms known to man – poetry.

This book is as much for the successful writers as it is for the marginalised. Yes we want great poets to enter (if they dare) but we also want to unleash the talent that lurks, untapped, just below the surface. We are all for the edgy, the outcast, the quirky but we also want the visionaries, the grafters and the committed. We want those who never get to make a living off grants or bursaries. For those who never win the big prize money or a publishing contract. This is a book for the people who write. If nothing else this anthology is a chance to know that you are good enough, that you can prosper and that your work is honest, refreshing and worthwhile.

The origins of the competition actually start way back in 1998 when I had just started teaching myself web design. As an avid poetry fan I envisaged an online competition where all could compete on an equal footing, but as I didn't know any famous writers back then, who would judge? And so my great literary *Endeavour* was sunk before it had first sailed.

Fast forward a few years and over a midnight pint at a creative writing class deep in the bowels of the south Wales valleys I happened to mention the idea to Welsh writer and poet John Evans who was instantly enthusiastic, supportive and generous in equal measure. John agreed to judge, I did the web site and the rest as they say is *in the past…*

1

Officially launched on St David's Day @ Clwb-Y-Bont, Pontypridd, 2007 the aim of the competition was to 'encourage and foster the wealth of creative writing talent that we know exists in Wales but somehow gets overlooked by the arts *business*'. We wanted to inspire people to capture real life in the present day not write about the artistic merits of a brick wall or electricity pylon. We aspired to give a voice to a new generation of poets and in this we believe we have succeeded. Less concerned with the purely academic types of literature we wanted to encourage free verse, experimentation, unique style, but above all raw passion.

With entries from Abu Dhabi to Australia, from Canada to China, from India to Israel, and from Kenya to Kuwait we have effortlessly reached out to the international market but it is understandably closer to home where we have had the greatest success with all the home nations, especially Wales, sending us most poems.

Our judges do the difficult, but hopefully rewarding task of reading every single entry and choosing the winners while I do the more mundane tasks. We get no grants, bursaries or funding from any external agencies whatsoever and so the continued support of poets through entry fees and our rabid word of mouth advertising is much appreciated.

In these, our early years, we've been very fortunate to have three fantastic judges:

First up is *Welsh Hero,* ex-punk rock star, writer, poet, filmmaker, environmentalist and activist John Evans. Second we have *Red Poet* Mike Jenkins, previous winner of the Wales Book of the Year and the John Tripp Award for Spoken Poetry and one of Wales' best poets. And third, crime novelist Sally Spedding, winner of the Forward Press Poetry Award, the Anne Tibble Poetry Prize, the Aesthetica Creative Works Competition and our very own 2010 prize.

So if anyone is foolish enough to doubt our credentials think again!

Why 20 winners I hear you ask? Well, the answer is simple. We want writers to know that they have impressed the judges. We want them to know that they can write, that they have something of value to say and in true democratic fashion the more voices the more powerful we become.

Certainly the poems in this collection tick the boxes. Love, death, pain and loss. Mythical, nostalgic, contemporary and lyrical. What they all have though is a subject close to the writers' heart and something that made the poet passionate enough to force them to put pen to paper or digits to a keyboard.

From the horrors of war to the majesty of a Horseshoe bat. From the loss of a child to climate change. From the raw wounds of sexual abuse to wise OAPs. From the Olympics to the Holocaust. We had poems about politics, a bus ride, the natural world, drug abuse, useless men, origami, our hometowns, a pet dog, history, modern day living, famous paedophiles and Mongolia to name just a few of the poets' subjects. But no matter the topic all of our winning poems touched our judges in some special way. We had rap, rhythm and rhyme. Sex, violence and humour. Sadness and joy. Shape and form. Often the use of language was sublime. And of course… *the passion, the passion, the passion, Mister Kurtz*!

I guess I must finish by saying how grateful I am to all the poets who so readily gave permission for their poems to be used, it is much appreciated. And so, to the anthology itself. The poems are divided into years, arranged winners first, followed by the judges' comments and then the specially commended entries.

The future? Well if the first five years are anything to go by we hope to continue in our quest to find new voices and look forward to the next five years with relish. We certainly have no plans to go away that's for sure. And finally, I hope you enjoy this collection as much as we have enjoyed reading your fantastic poems.

Dave Lewis, July 2011

The 2007 Winners
Judged by John Evans

Concrete by Gavin Price

Con construct, nae lay deified, serpentine eye belie bitter ego
Denied, satiate and purify chase.
Lick batteries not pylons
Likely geezers selling nylons in the lanes,
they all stink of old spilled spunk,
crusty gunk, sticking vile to their long johns,
she don't suck that hard for no one or no stocking,
saliva slopped in the ginnel gutter,
she tossed him off he finger fucked her,
pope don't mind so long as dick don't linger,
he drank beer she drank cider,
that's apple juice to you.
Lights, powerless observe mutely,
behind blackouts the keen and the curious hide,
think they can tell a stranger from shadow,
but cant tell their arse from their elbow,
doodle bugs come and do them good,
fall and flatten their comfy homes,
shake and rattle their rattling stoves,
as they cook up crack for a car boot sale,
e-bay or some other god forsaken trading hole.
She spat her teeth as she went of her feet,
ripped from head to twat by a sword on the wall,
uncle Billy saved from the paws of a kraut,
must have been a general or fancy dressed contestant,
either way dead as dead old fuck now,
sing songs to keep them whole and sane,
aim at the base and exclaim to the tone,
of an ever flat marching band,
"granny got fucked in old johnnies shed
if grampy finds out they'll both be dead
granny got rimmed, Johnny got head

7

on the blob, he did her arse instead
because were fucking for a better time
were fucking for a better life
were fucking, were fucking"
but they dont sing fuck they sing
"um tiddly um pum, pum pum"
if you don't like the taste don't swallow
old Chinese saying,
"don't be a cunt and you wont get fucked"
Old man sage says
"there's a snake in my spine"
Zen says
"   "

the Buddha just smiles,
realises its not quite a cry but close enough
stretch your legs Susie girl,
stretch em wide and give us a twirl,
Oh John be honest son,
you twist your charm and turn out scum,
when the law strikes you down,
you'll try your wit and half a crown,
but unbought the time will stamp
Seven times seven and cast you out
Oh Johnny boy don't you know
War, make beasts of us all.

My Body is Old Porridge by Eloise Williams

Now that I am thirty five
On honest reflection in the mirror
Without motive I can say, my body is old porridge.

Tits. Two (statistically I'm grateful). Gloopy.
Humungous gurgling roll where stomach used to be.
A sight that brings a globule of puke hacking. Hanging. Congealing.
Tasteless. Thankless.
Insipid.

Arse. A moon with craters.
Men don't want to land.
There is a nose. Pocked. Crusted. Smelling sickly smells.

Heart clogged. Lumpen.
I am overall grey.
Recycling, though commendable, impossible in this case.
There is an indescribable scent. Pungent.
Years of stewing. Steeped in whisky. Ingredients stirring.

Fingers wooden, splintered, sharp
Itching to scour away spiteful skin. Scratching yellow, blue and
    brown.
Vagina (I am old enough to say that now) glued together. A skin
    formed over. Pasted.
    Virginity regained. Unwanted.

Every so often sour jam, clotted, warm. A reminder of failure.
My use and use by date passing.
Yearnings. Put a lid on.
Bingo wings shake jelly like
Only to distract from deeper thoughts.

Despairing bubble eyes. Steel scorched and scarred.
Yes. I can hide it.
Smiling tightly. A shrill escape of gas.

Put away the glass.
Of the inside out.
Rockets. Shooting, steaming, simmering, exploding. Steaming,
   piping, sparking hot.
Remembering love and childhood laughter. Sweetened.
Impish ideals. Idiosyncrasies. Intelligence. Condensed.

Dreams, boundless, endless, new.
Grateful. Thankful.
Eloquence evaporated. Afraid of escape through rotting yellow
   teeth.

space by Amanda Weeks

He left a space.
Never knew he was a "he" until the post mortem.
The little life. I never saw his face.
A tiny body. A huge space.

He left a void.
It couldn't be filled with drink or drugs
Believe me, I tried.
Six months' gestation. Eternal void.

He left guilt.
Was I wrong to decorate his room,
Buy a pram with matching quilt?
Three pounds, two ounces. Heavy guilt.

He left despair.
A freak with bad insides
A child I could not bare.
Neo-natal death. Life of despair.

He left me
Alone with my bottle and pills
And people saying it wasn't meant to be.
A wanted son. He left me.

Judges' comments:

Concrete, by Gavin Price

An excellent poem. Filled with the sound, rhythms, and musical qualities of language. Alliteration, and assonance, pushing each line along relentlessly. The mind is drawn onwards, and onwards, towards meaning, towards an end; each point picked up and qualified by a clause or phrase, then thrown down to be picked up again later; the language creating a speed and urgency, as we move at times beyond meaning, and a refusal to let this jaggedness slow us down. There is no gap between his words and the world. Poetic utterance at its very best, and a very worthy competition winner. From doodlebugs, to E-bay, to Buddha..."War makes beasts of us all". Poetry will only survive as a relevant art form if voices like Gavin Price are heard more often.

My Body Is Old Porridge, by Eloise Williams

Another excellent poem, finely observed and executed. A female voice speaks with candour about the changes and bodily experiences of the aging process. Making use of the subtle effects of sound, which contrast wonderfully with the matter of fact, frankness, and sometimes harsh way the poet addresses the reader, and herself. "On honest reflection in the mirror". Yet there is humour in this self-portrait, "Arse. A moon with craters. Men don't want to land", and all the complexities of emotion are addressed, "Of the inside out. Rockets. Shooting, steaming, simmering, exploding". This poem by Eloise Williams would win many competitions. Poem as creative art. Another poet whose voice needs to be heard.

space, by Amanda Weeks

Again, an excellent example of how poetry should be written in the twenty-first century. There is no pretension, both language and subject matter speak directly to the reader. The speaker faces the pain of miscarriage, "He left a space. Never knew he was a "he" until the post mortem. The little life. I never saw his face." Loss. Mourning. Pain. Self-doubt. Difficult subjects. Nothing is dodged or ducked. Are all tackled head on. "He left despair. A freak with bad insides. A child I could not bare." The use of rhythm and the subtleties of rhyme are expertly crafted. Amanda Weeks is another poet who has a finely tuned ear for the aural patterning of language. Honest, open, and deeply moving, a poem which thoroughly deserves its place among the competition winners. More please.

John Evans, August, 2007

Specially Commended, 2007

Her hairs not short by Gavin Price

Her hairs not short, unless torn is short,
she bleeds like time when times not taught.
◎No selfish lie cloud her eye,
no false loathe make her cold.

Top estate tantrums she ever views,
Bottom feeders upon the concrete shore,
She won't buy no faith,
her faiths an unpaid chore.

She screams inside, inside ostrich cries,
pillows draw her head subside and she lies,
fear is never a plan well made,
the moon is only half a day

In peace contempt takes wings,
Pity dreams of freedom, compassion so sweet,
"Tender, tender, tender ill
tender take me away to still"

In godless days in a box bedroom,
she ponders, obscure those days of Jude,
the meaning, meaningless of Ecclesiastes
sudden in truth she short in grasp.

All these days turned so gentle on,
she lays shaded as the sun beats pulsing out,
a window ajar, a half made patio terrace,
half drunk tea and warm cold compress◎.

She's a tortoise in a shell suit
Battered lush like old bruised fruit,
vine buckled and bent loose in skin,
knows no possession, owns no the sin

Where's her beau when paramours fail,
her gallant knight in shining foil,
horse for the silent kingdoms trade,
⊚jousts the spectres, spirits assails⊚.

A vapour so thick, so thinly strewn,
the strangest bloom blossoms mercy,
warrior flora of sweet release
effervescent she breaths to swollen.

In her mind the romance yearns,
of lovers laughing waltzing turns⊚,
the sun breaks through her damp cold walls
her knees grow tougher with every fall.

This could be the last time
could be the first for evermore,
her flesh it scratches like old vinyl
and skips back in this loop eternal

Her hairs not short unless, unless torn is short
Frets of life they run well worn
there ain't no need but still she stills,
never quite feels the love she fills.

Solar Plexus by Jane Fox

Dropped the tree rootless for Christmas Judas no burial sound
    intentions
Bark blight black spotted jigsaw puzzle perfect-fit linoleum yellow
    cellular
Lift linoleum walnut shell spent feast fattened beast
Damp foot scrape singular lime diamond sparkle standing tiny
Carpet green rain gems lovelier than worn on any hand
Eager eyes closed look further than fingers

Hoover horses snuffling synchronised mowing mission twin coats
    and colours
Next field forgotten uncoated ragged trims
Leaning into fence to warmer brothers greener pastures nose to
    grindstone
Ten-hour working day no head lift loitering daydream bellybutton
    gaze
Creatures beautiful as they are serious no head for rub or scratch
We have work to do we will clean up a whole field in one shift

Hurry to notice bellybag cancer-coming coma operate separate
    stomachs
Give trolley belly break bursting brim-band stagger burgeoning
    aisles
Squeeze vessels blood flesh through to skin bags belly bags arse bags
Eyes bulging no longer bigger than belly Outsize no size too big
Snort chatter grass greener stand at fence watch Race hoover
    overstretched dead

No size too small We all gain weight if we eat
Black boned under black flesh bulging bellies
Hungry when mother comes back
I'm a child mother and need to eat

19

I like it
My sister a child also, needs to eat
I want my dinner We all want dinner
Are you fat enough to hold a ring let me see your fingers
Push through bars skinny finger-bones bigger knuckles
You'll never wear diamonds
Doesn't remember how she fed me

Flights of Fancy by Richard Garman

I saw the black-speckled pom-pom plume rise.
My mind wrestled with words and metaphors to capture the image
Many had become one, the one had infinity - there was no entity to capture
One dunlin is a waddling, gobbling wader, a flock is a giant jellyfish on wings
A wheeling, swirling, metamorphosing, light-controlling swarm, painting its presence
on the evening sky. An unseen hand throws a morsel of flock to the ground, the parent ball
re-forms and rolls on. Discarded drifters bounce off the seashore, coalescing back into the bosom
of the group. A mushroom dome forms on the horizon. A trunkless tree peers over the sea, then
Macbeth like, uproots from Birnam and shuffles down the shore to Dunsinane. The canopy of
leaves and branches waves in the wind transforming into a swarm of bees or a speechless
comic bubble begging an answer to its unspoken question. Order! Order!
The motion is proposed, seconded by the bird with the
speckled breast. No need to vote
Carried unanimously
We roost
down
-
here

In 1968, in the thin air of Mexico City, Mongolia's first silver medal was won by Munkhbat Jigjidym in the middleweight (up to 87kg) freestyle wrestling by John Gallas

('World Sports' magazine)

The air up
here is woozy,
shallow, sweet,
but not so ... um
head-clear.
Clear up a green, high, home hill,
bear-tangled with wind, the here-air
heartens my head. Up and down a numb,
bleach mat, hugging souls here, souls that

bow	grass down, that clog	clouds,
that	wilt wind a whole day's	horse
ride.	*I eat all comers, faces*	*like*
bubbles	*in new cheese, muscled*	*as milk*
and	*wrestling shadows : keep*	*hold*

of what is bad, boy, and throw

it down. The air	up here is
woozy, shallow,	sweet, but not
so ...um head-clear.	One foot, one grab
out ! up ! down !	a numb, bleach mat.
Falls on all this	green, high, home
hill. Hold what	is bad, and down.
Sleep and	*live with*
it hidden	*and held.*
The air	*is clear*
sweet : take it	*down to what*
it is. I hold	my own soul,
that hangs on my	*belt while I sing.*

22

Balancing Mixed Vegetables On A Motorway Bridge
by Clive Gilson

Fergus vomits in the street.
Walking to the pub he stops
and deposits bile in the gutter.
"Better out..." he says.
Fergus walks miles out of his way
to find a bridge over the ring road
and urged on by boys who admire
the calculated insanity of the man,
he climbs onto the safety rail
and walks backwards with his eyes shut.
None of the boys can tear their eyes
away from road kill fascination.
Fergus shouts and cracks a smile.
The boys grin and shout back,
in thrall to the image of a body
lying fifty feet below them.
The trick is being in control,
balancing the weight of possibility
against their lack of imagination.
The boys are sick in the gutter,
depositing small rivers of Tetley's
finest ale down the drains.

Fragments of Cardiff by Kate Scarratt

Tidal.
A place I
come to,
go from, can't
stay in.
The rivers once
boasted
tides, now
a barrage.
But I
have reclaimed my tides, letting
them
wash me. Transports of delight,
means of escape,
of discovery.
In Cardiff I have
dreams
I take home with
me.

Unbowed.
Cardiff's bloody wet
full of bloody puddles
bloody cars and buses driving through
them.
Bloody chip papers,
dog shit
drunks
A place where people cry out
strangely
in the night.
Full of bloody -

life.

Corporate Cardiff
Corporate, corporate, Cardiff,
Corporate, corporation, co-operation, corporate,
constipation,
Corporate, incorporation,
Corporate, corpuscle,
Corporate, cormorant,
Cor! Cardiff.

Cardiff
 Windy rainy arcaded contradictory:
 villages and monoliths,
 civic pride and the Big Issue
 castles and culture and
clubs (and banks which are now pubs), and the man with a sax and a
dog
 outside Boots'
 So come on now boyos let's
 not hurt our brains,
 let's all
get hammered down the Ferret and Radiator and
have a
bloody good time.

Did you know?
You can see the stars, like,
from the middle of Cardiff.

If they turn the lights
off.

On Eric Gill - typophile etc. by Emily Hinshelwood

A: Gill Sans
160 miles from Bedlam. Tucked
in sham-Gothic God-house. Four families
and a quotient of neurotics. Secluded.

There's stone galore for the taking
waterfalls for naked bathing and all garments
are rough-knitted - the colour of sheep.

He lounges, legs sprawled, nothing
on but a knee-length cassock. Your
affectionate brother in St. Dominic.

B: Golden Cockerel Roman
He shaped our interface with words:
shaved, smoothed curves, pressed fonts.

As Golden Cockerel he puffed and crowed,
kept the coop, with eyes keen and unkempt hair.
While hens were scratching, clucking, plucking
he, with footrule, measured the I (up and down)
how wide the legs of a V should spread
(the O contracting), where the Q is pierced.
And cast all things on the rock that is Christ.

C: Floriated Capitals
He resented the freedom of plants:
they dance their flowers full-frontal
in the hedges; a symphony of lust, poke
stiff and garish from parted petals, dripping
scent, enflamed and shameless.
We adorn our dining tables with

vases of fresh-cut scarlet lips,
rigid male thrusting,
and it doesn't put us off our food.
So why, he asks, are men
to hide their precious decor, tucked
sideways into trousers, dishonoured
and neglected?

D: Perpetua

I read snatches of his diaries.
About his daughters. Perhaps
most chilling is his matter of
factness. The briefness of his
records: Date. The hole he
enters. How long he spends.

To: Orpheus@lyre.com by Kate Noakes

You total prat! What on earth
were you thinking?
That's the problem isn't it,
you weren't, on earth
or thinking.

Did you really expect me
not to follow you?
You made a deal and Hades
is nothing if not a god
of his word, damn it.

I could cheerfully strangle
you myself, if only I could
reach my bony fingers
through the soil and
round your neck.

Thanks a lot for leaving
me stranded down here
with these half-people
and dogs who go around
all day moaning.

And what are you doing,
wandering about feeling
sorry for yourself? It's no party
for me and most of all,
I hate pomegranates.

Urban Tales by Phil Knight

Urban Jack and Urban Jill
Struggled up a fucking hill
to get a rock or two of crack
but when they got there
the fucking Cops were there
and the little fuckers got a smack.

Little Miss Muffit
Shat on her tuffit
smoking some sweat cocaine
then down come a spider
who sat down beside her
that said
"It's society what's to blame".

There was an old woman
who lived in a shoe
she had sold everything else
to pay for her drug habit.

The Grand old Duke of York
had ten thousand men
and the less said about him
              the better.

Swansea Bay Promenade, 22nd May 2005 by Isobel Norris
(it's about quarter to three)

It smells of salt (from the stormflung seawater, and
Marie-Eve's crisps), Kris' leather-hugged sweat, Hann's perfume
(Calvin Klein: Scene). It's raining - that's all I can
feel; my hair is wet down the back of my shirt; our hands
are slipping each other. Again. My tongue is wet
with ready salted rain; the ocean spray; old, used sand.
There's nothing to be seen beyond this
cast of characters - the sky and sea are the same
stone, sea-wall grey. There's the flash of Jen's camera
(that I think is lightning), the wind that's stripping us,
Hannah's laughter, this new kid on the block (the thunder),
a car horn, and the lot of them running to catch us up,
their feet pounding - DO YOU WANT SOME CHIPS?
NO, I say, NO (because all I want is this).

Bags by Roger Barnett

Windblown, the Asda bag explores the car park.
Sometimes floating high as a helium jellyfish.
Sometimes scraping along briefly on hard tarmac.
Like me, searching for shelter, safety.

Vehicles' underbellies provide a dark haven.
Mud-streaked wheels court rubber shields,
Protection against short-sighted moggies
And piss-take canines.
Like me, aware of danger.

Whooping, a Tesco holdall hurricanes into view,
Scatterbrained and vibrant dipped.
Swaying close, giving a plastic wink,
The bag flashes a curvaceous handle.
Like me, looking for romance.

Asda balloons like a blushing peacock.
Feels the skin stretch and harden.
Cruising the thermal currents,
Tesco thrusts and bobs,
Dances alongside, mouth wide.
Like me, craving seduction.

Suddenly a trolley lady pounces
On her precious prey.
Places them slickly in a tattered pocket,
Joining her carrier community,
Flirting and caressing forever.
Like me, true companions.

What I am by Carrie-Ann Fry

I'm the type of person that reads the last page first
I'm the girl who believes in the very worst
I'm the one who makes a wish knowing it won't come true
I'm the idiot who falsifies the saying "fool proof"
I'm the person walking with no coat in the rain
I'm the psycho that cuts herself, just to feel that pain
I'm the one that cries for lost love inside
I'm also the one that lets you take her for a ride
I'm the sleazy one you want but don't need
I'm an infected cut that continues to bleed
I'm the rumour you hate to think might be true
I'm the dog shit stuck to your brand new shoe
I'm everything bad
Because I'm nothing to you.

Inside Out by Anthony Keating

February
In a seaside cafe.

Somewhere out there,
Though the lace and condensation,
There is a down at heal town,
Aching for the picture postcard past,
That a lick of paint has failed to reignite.

Miles apart
across a corner table,
A couple
try to escape themselves,
Yet nurse the soft pulse of enmity
that throbs between them.
Their teaspoons clattering
with broken promises.

As they like the town
wonder,
Why with so much history
do they have so little now?

Connecting by Leah Armstead

Voices in the dark hours, just TV,
are trapped in the thin walls between us,
a paper bearing stories I can't decipher.

Talking, gunshot, screaming—
⊚all a faked violence, merely play.
It interferes with my dreaming.

Weeping, hassled talking, cars screeching
through the walls, through the long night,
in the pressing, wordless heat.

This is a tale of sleepless neighbours,
mysterious banging about, rousing sounds—
⊚and no way to actually speak to each other.

No way to communicate with you,
to ask for silence and the freedom
to sleep in a silence only birds know.

We are so close, and yet there is this distance
that stretches endlessly between us.
Only garbled noise connects us.

Extinction by Cerys Jones

Heads leaning, lips parting, eyes closing –
I thought this would make things easier.

Tongues entering, tastes changing, heart racing -
Yet all I can think of is us.

Shirt ripping, belt unbuckling, bra snapping -
Why did you have to end it?

Fingers entering, hand enclosing, skin sweating -
I don't want to be here.

Bodies fucking, teeth clenching, moans heightening -
Oh God how did it end up like this?

Him climaxing, me crying, you oblivious
That for me, it will never be the same.

The Size Zero Debate by Emma Sullivan

The reflection in the mirror that I see,
Strangely seems to rain down on me
The eyes that I hold are blind
Everything halting to a tantamount grind.
The images that we portray,
Must have some affect don't they?
Confine us all to imperfection,
Enabling us all to feel disconnection.
They say that it's culturally relevant,
But somehow I feel dependent,
On the notion that I see,
How I wish I could be free.
Unable to be original,
I spend my life being cynical.
Despairing at the lack of hope,
Wash my face with an endless amount of soap.
How can I ever be good enough?
In a society which thinks like this.
Surely there is somewhere that I can go,
Where I can belong - who knows?

Bus Ride by Josiah Rowlands

Bus ride, bus ride, bus, bus, bus,
Look at us, look at us,
Riding on a bus.
We go fast, we go slow,
Now we stop and now we go.
That's enough.
Let's get off.

The 2008 Winners
Judged by John Evans

Visually-speaking by Emily Hinshelwood

Non gave birth to St David during a storm in about AD462. Her holy well is renowned for curing eye-diseases. The poem was written during an adjournment of a public inquiry about a community wind farm.

I've been stuck in the chamber too long with dead
breath doing the rounds between "yes wind farm",
"no wind farm and don't wreck a speck of my grass
or the planet will shrink to pea-sized piss".

I've been stuck in the chamber too long with "turbines
kill my world – I'll crack my balls before I let them step
an inch towards my precious fossil fuelled, polluted palace
on the hill" – "oh, and if the wind farm's built…
I'll never get to paint again".

I've been stuck…
struck by "climate change poo poo"
by "nobody has a right to mess with *my* view"
by "what about the dead poet who
loved
this
spot?"

And today I walk
St Non's Bay
- she who cured the eye yet now
has the view of
towers puking clouds up and outwards.

I've been stuck in the chamber too long with mud-stuck plod;
with "wind farms look like bog brushes – kill our birds, sheep
horses, fish and children"; with "wind farms fizz our brains and

bring the psychos out"; with wind farms look like manic crucifixions
and don't forget what happened to Jesus".

So I throw a penny into Non's Well –
after all she gave us David
p'raps she'll sort out climate change as well.

Polyfiller by Clare Ferguson-Walker

A pinioned point held between then and tomorrow,
windows looking out over space contorted by conditions.
Conditions manifested, immortalized as memory.
A quick fumbling in a paint peeling doorway,
tasted like fags, dry pussy needed some spit,
thirteen year old tits, posing as a bird from "Mayfair"
a scene under dads bed,
we consumed it, thought we was to be consumed.
Over painted lips bigger than real,
leaving kisses on pints, rings on cocks.
Checking out the comp. down the local, she's here,
sends me pouring over the eyelined eyes,
mirror that's reflected a whole teetering inadequacy, many faces.
Biology, mind you, natures way to fight in the gene pool,
bikini mud wrestling for the best cum.
Farcical joinings, always the actress, some cuts through though,
dad never kissed me.
Back on the razz, commando for the lads,
a chimp with a red arse, screaming, fuck me now,
just one more and it'll sort me out,
spunk like polyfiller, congealing in the crack.
Gave new age a go, crystals, ganj, throat warbling charms,
God within, not without, my body, the cock, consorting with the air.
I am my own father, mother too, the whole extended family, dog and
all,
the universe is one, a knife point sharpened on a lonely stone.

One.

A glass submarine though, cracked with too much depth,
washed up in a cell, padded with some shit crust on the wall.
All technicolour dream coat and no knickers,

syringes of Parkinson shakes, shook me down to the baby,
pushed out with a loving scream, dad visited and kissed me.
"Settled" now though, the mud,
thick layer at the bottom of a clearer river.
Porn pages float aloft, pert tits just visible under a ripple.
Still want the knife though, worms in the mud see.
A slash here, a severing tuck there,
30 year old tits now, suckled twice,
no worms in the milk I pray.

I don't do hugs by Eloise Williams

I don't do hugs.
Claustrophobic.
Enveloping circles.

When you say love there's a vacuum.

I don't mind fucking.
Blindfolded.

You suck your fingers in readiness
though some holes can never be filled.

Life precariously tilts and judders
under a savage blood moon.

Naughty girl.
Half heartedly.

Embarrassment hangs on the air.

Lust makes your face a cruelty.
Mouth stretching to odd angles.
Wept oceans for your smile.

Yet now I'm encrusted in sores.

A smack goes by without comment.
I guess you read a text book.
"How to be Dirty – Part I".

Twat.
Dry.

Uncooperative.
The body shuns the head.

But shattered is an overused word.

Bruise around my nipple.
Proof that I belong.
Human detritus.
Ravaged
in a sea of sweat and spunk.

Visually-speaking, by Emily Hinshelwood

A wonderful poem with fine lyric qualities and a worthy winner. It cleverly highlights the dilemmas we now face in relation to global warming and the need for sustainable energy – and the fact that the poem focuses on those issues here, Wales, now, today, makes it all the more relevant. As the poem suggests, there are no quick fix, easy answers – if there are any at all – and it is filled with that frustration. The poet cleverly uses the repetition of reported and direct speech, with slight changes, to build and build momentum, urging the reader forwards: "yes wind farm, / no wind farm and don't wreck a speck of my grass / or the planet will shrink to pea-sized piss". While the use of line-breaks, one word lines, and excellent imagery ("towers puking clouds up and outwards") in the middle stanza's skillfully slow the pace and perception, allowing the reader to pause for breath and reflect. History is here too, as the poet cleverly weaves the past with the present: "And today I walk / St Non's Bay / – she who cured the eye..." The rhythm quickens again as frustration grows, and form skillfully matches content, until we reach a breathless flourish: "wind farms look like bog brushes – kill our birds, sheep / horses, fish and children"; "with wind farms fizz our brains and bring the psychos out". No pastoral idyll. No romantic seascape, this. The natural landscape has become a challenger rather than a comforter. A nice "view" has become an environmental, ideological, and aesthetic, conundrum. NIMBY vs. Planet Earth. "I'll crack my balls before I let them step / an inch towards my precious fossil fuelled, polluted palace on the hill". Congratulations to Emily Hinshelwood, a poet Highly Commended in last years competition, on producing a topical work of such high quality.

Polyfiller, by Clare Ferguson-Walker

This poem reminds me why, of all the art forms, poetry is perhaps my favourite. No film, painting, or piece of music could really do this – could really adequately convey the mixture of the concrete and abstract, interior and exterior, of yesterday and today. Pollyfiller, is poetic form teetering on a precipice. Language stretched to the limit. The shifting syntax reveals, and brings into consequence, the various orders of experience, allowing each to arise from and transform what came before it. In this manner no position remains static or gains ascendancy and none controls the direction of what follows. Life: "A pinioned point held between then and tomorrow"; flickering on walls; "in a paint peeling doorway"; "under dad's bed"; "down the local". The poem is dark, dangerous, gritty, and unpredictable. An open sore. A wound. A "knife point sharpened on a lonely stone". It affects the reader on a physical level, making them uncomfortable – and that's always a good thing. "A glass submarine though, cracked with too much depth, / washed up in a cell, padded with some shit crust on the wall. / All technicolour dream coat and no knickers,...".

In a world of samey-sameness, and poor imitations of the past, this is a fresh, original, and truly inspirational piece of work. So, Polyfiller, then. Like last year's winning entry, another poem which may upset the Arts Council and our self-appointed poetry elite. Thank fuck for good art, then. Thank fuck for Clare Ferguson-Walker. Vive la resistance.

I don't do hugs, by Eloise Williams

Excellent poem. Excellent title. "I don't do hugs". Very, now. Today. A love poem for the disaffected, disconnected, SMS messaging, Wii exercising, iPod generation. Lust over love. Fetishism over flowers. "You suck your fingers in readiness / though some holes can never be filled". The poem is very skilfully laid out on the page, with very well thought out use of line breaks. Each word hangs in the air for a moment. Each line abrupt, a slap in the face. "Twat. / Dry. / Uncooperative. / The body shuns the head." Every word used in this poem was given an impressive amount of consideration. Every punctuation mark, every line break, every time the poet has chosen to use a new stanza... counts. The staccato rhythm of the piece, forces the reader to pause, forces them to consider, forces them to contemplate, and draws them in physically, and emotionally, to the dark and unsettling side of human relations today. "Naughty girl. / Half heartedly. Embarrassment hangs on the air." The poet 's use of imagery is also very well crafted and executed. Again, not a single word wasted. No unnecessary adjectives. "Mouth stretching to odd angles. / Wept oceans for your smile." The poem drags the reader along, through this world of "How to be Dirty...", until they reach it's moving and powerful conclusion: "Bruise around my nipple. / Proof that I belong. / Human detritus. / Ravaged / in a sea of sweat and spunk."

A great poem in a world of bland, meaningless, versification, and another top three entry from the talented, Eloise Williams.

John Evans, August, 2008

Specially Commended, 2008

On deck with Alun Lewis, the secret sleeper by Owen Lowery

A vast expiration of lucid stars
new and uncluttered by light's noise, ageless
by his terms, quivers darkly above him,
unfolds a languid arm, a cold caress.

His subconscious voice succumbs, relaxes,
absorbs the slow percussion of the sea,
the warm thrum of turbines, plate-steel clenching,
the night gushing its refreshing sweetness.

He'll whisper as much in his letter home
and immerse in his old familiar pain,
knowingly and deliberately confuse
Cwmaman's heavy hills with the contours

of each undiscovered land. Faces blend
degrees of separation. A brown girl
flexes by a brothel wrapped in Welsh vowels,
the New World's eyes stare whiteness from the mines

and the tireless pit-wheels of his dreaming.
He'll save his last thought for the flimsy deck.
He'll let the rancid stink of the troopship
slip quietly through his fingers, his secret

guarded by the round hull of a lifeboat.
It's conceivable he *was* felt soft-shoed
and in shorts passing through the sleeping men
to lie stripped above, turn grey with the moon,

if not by the lads triple-tiered in bunks,
then by the ancient hand of the spectre

who shakes him to himself in the morning
to douse the place he lay with clean water.

Trout by James Gower

The rainbow trout that's on my plate
A captive farm-ed battery fish
Was sucked from mum by a pipette
And pumped onto a warm lab dish.

It never knew the river bed
Or played in streams but grew too fat
And led a life routinely fed
Inside a gleaming factory vat.

And, when Tescos said 'twas so
My teenage trout with all his mates
Were measured and allowed to grow
Outside in rubber man made lakes

He never basked, leapt, loved or spawned
Engaged in nature's repartee
But died alone. No brothers mourned.
Laid out in plastic for my tea.

Forget-Me-Not by Leah Ebdon

Every word a scalpel
slashing violent
hexagonal patterns.
I'm motionless.
Tiny flushes of red burst,
soak through cotton,
the dress I wore today
for you.
Each delicate little forget-me-not
blushes red
and I stand
drenched in hatred.

Hide by Jane Galletly

An accident waiting nine months to happen
A warm olive in your arms
My androgynous skin cling filmed
Presenting a clear performance
A small breathing building
Housing my interior architecture
Growing into myself and my older sister's jeans.
Wearing your purple paisley of scars
An index of hidden harm
Search my flesh for clues
A carpet burn... a bruise?
I am held together
Like the air holds a kite,
Light.

Learning from Buzzards by Roger Elkin

Recall those dust-dry physics classes
with magnets and iron filings which jigged
into elliptical patterns that demarked polarity;
so these buzzards are pulled magnetically
towards each other as working in pairs
they swipe clear the sky's windowpane.

Like poles repel; unlike attract

Raggy wing-tips splay-fingering, they soar:
circling, and circling – nearer, nearer, near –
the sun's trapeze artists swinging into exchanges
      her / him   him / her

Like poles repel; unlike attract

From beneath they're Angels of the North, arms
outspread: or prototypes for death's-head hawk-moths
even down to the carpal darkness-targets
on their wings making a second set of eyes
to nail these landscapes down.

Their slow-flapping, broad-wing sailing
seems aimlessly lazy; but that's illusion:
they're quartering the groundscape in careless
carefulness, fixed with all the attentiveness
of one whose gaze is dragged, magnetized,
to a deformed face. They cannot unleash eyes.

Like poles repel; unlike attract

Bent on survival, every second is counting:

they sweep copses, hedgerows, moor lines, heaths
for fledglings, voles, shrews, beetles.
Imagine the visual precision that allows
the picking off of beetles from a stooped
headlong-down pounce.
What angle-calculation.
What poise.

> *The radius of curvature*
> *is twice the focal length*

And, at roost, doze with one eye closed
trying to work out how on earth
the laws of gravity can be justified.

Watching Layers Form by Jenny Adamthwaite

We watch New Year cut through the ribbon from the sofa.
The clock above the mantle piece heaves the weight of Last Year like

a

ball

and

chain.

Your watch is a minute ahead, you say
as you try to stare out time, gripping each second
in case the year bolts past so fast you never get to see its face.

I notice for the first time the shape of your hands,
how fragile they look,

how used,

how tired.

Pen-y-Fan Revisited by Christopher Rogers

At the bottom.
Parked up ate a bacon roll
Considered chilli marinade,
Plumped for brown sauce, tried the tea, had one sip,
But soon there was none left for me.
Tried to talk her into another day
My Aunt Ann's and lunch and biscuits less than half an hour away.
But steadfast.
Resolute.
From Efail Isaf to boot.
Dill was taking no such flannel.
So off we went.
Up to Pen-y-Fan.
Hell.

Half way up.
Coming down, Nordic sticks, no skis.
A lady hiker.
"Ooo, it's harder coming down... the knees,
But the view up there is sure to please".
Dill just took my hand.
The smile.
The squeeze.
Little people.
Like ants, above and ants below, by the bacon roll and tea van.
A little closer now.
A little clearer,
Pen-y-Fan.

At the top.
We hugged and ate duck eggs, marvelled at Mumbles
And the Steepholm Island.

Clear across the Beacons north,
Hugged again and felt it worth
The while to have come so far without the dirty,
smoky car.
We spoke to a sheep,
To the edge did creep,
Watched a glider's steep
And soaring flight.
Looked forward to a night,
Post bath,
of restful sleep
and then came down from those prehistoric seas.
And you know what?
It wasn't so bad on the knees

So thank you Dill.
For helping me with my smoking ban.
And my first trip for 34 years to that beacon of south Wales,
That outdoor "Innocent Smoothie" of a mountain
Pen-y-Fan.

Barry Island revisited by Emyr Jones

Let's go to Barry Island dad
And sit out in the sun.
Let's go to Barry Island dad
Perhaps we'll have some fun.
Let's go to Barry Island dad
I'll take you in your chair,
And maybe you'll remember
The time you took me there.

Boireann by Graham Burchell

They are both old
Boireann and her

she wants to remain in the car

hunched

regarding the other
through the smear of a window

the intrusion of a wing mirror mars
a romance of meddled limestone

a partial view
yet she is content

because she sees

even when these days
rooks overhead look crimson

one colour among several is lost

and edges soften

I am younger
not as young as clouds blowing off the Atlantic
older than wild rose or bloody cranesbill
growing in the clints and grikes
of Boireann otherwise Boirinn
this Burren *great rock* frac-
tured

like *her* calcium-leached spine

osteoporosis of the karst

Show me the money by Amanda Weeks

Thirty million quid.
Thirty million quid.
The arts council of Wales
Gets thirty million quid.
Every year from the taxpayer
That's you and me
And gamblers
That's people who play the lottery.

They give bursaries to writers –
Academi. Apparently
But they're usually established –
So nothing for you. And bugger all for me.

And they organise writing competitions
If you can afford the entry fees
And write in a style that pleases geriatric judges
Don't' know about you, but that's not me.

Thirty million quid.

Bronze sculptures of urban myths
Soaked in piss, outside KwikSave in Mountain Ash,
It all costs cash.

Thirty million quid.

Readings by Academi bigwigs
For free. Although they pay themselves a fat fee
And use the opportunity to force their books
Onto the likes of you and me.
But what about the struggling writers,

Who don't want to sell their soul
Who live in the real world
Who don't kiss arse and don't write about coal?

I'll tell you what we get. Poetry and Pints.
It's free.
Well, it would be. It's only you and me
Reading poetry. And who the hell are we?
We're not worthy of a bursary.

So I'll read my poems and have a pint
Which I'll pay for myself because the Arts Council's too tight.
After all they only get... how much?
Thirty million quid, that's right.

Union Cat by Patricia Bellotti

I do like a nice bolshie cat. Ours
is called Blod and her soul is red
red as the Square. When she came to us she
had the cats' unionspeak by heart:
To each according to his needs – and
by God did she need! The other bit
From each… is not yet part
of her understanding, but in her manner
she repays.

Times she drives me mad:
her other name is Cooking Fat
and when I scream it at her
she bristles her scorn at me, yawns,
indulges in a little obscene washing. Sometimes
turns her back on me, tail aloft, giving
a quick flash of her bottom eye (though
I am as Welsh as she is) before
snaking through the cat-flap to convene
the caterwaul congress. As usual, she
opens the proceedings:
Everybody out!

But come evening, fed and restored to peace,
we are sisters; I toast my toes,
we watch *Pobl y Cwm*, and now that
I have reached the age I am and a measure
of compromise is agreed
her purring matches my heartbeat.

Flies on Coke by Ellie Madden

Quiet first, the party.
Glitchy conversations,
pools of 'smalltalk'.
Stultified!

In comes social lubricant,
cheap wine,
noise rises, people spill things,
and laugh,
people eat and touch more.

Later
nervous
young men
in trendy jeans
become visible
and animated
(there is one
who is tense.
His wife
has gone
to fuck
another).
I am kissed
and adored
…for microseconds…
before
another piece
comes into
ever scanning eyes.
Then

they are gone.
Flies.
Erratic.
Self fulfilling
focus.

A woman is bemused
when two men, who had been chatting,
suddenly disappear behind a corner.
'They've gone to take coke' I say.
'Oh' she sighs.
'I wondered why they'd been so interested'.

As the night continues
the flies keep up the pace
Full of seemingly heartfelt focus
in each other's
shit.

The next day, on the drive, I find
a broken glass and £20, rolled up
with snot and dirt on it.
I use it to pay for lunch
shared with a bemused woman!

on Davaar Island by John Gallas

for Patti

This man *is* an island; whose crooked mole
I dare to cross, writing as I go. My pencil in the rain.

His stone way is put on the sea maybe to try us.
I – I write this word as I – *sqwunch* on damn-cracked shell bones
and the seaweed skins of late, exploded sinners,
some of them with tails, who did not thrive.

And I'm still writing.

Searched while I scribble nearer. His island-head
not quite out to the eyes, but green and judgement still.

I rock-hop round to Crucifixion Cave.
I will write this letter in mid-air –
C

And at its mouth a gasping goat, glue-eyed,
hair-slubbed and pink-distended,
maybe with some devil's thing
to resurrect the drying damned;
those angels' midge-revolt.

The Jesus picture is not very good.

But He is already everywhere.
My father fiercely unbelieved. My mother could not say Never.
Grandma saw angels. Granddad sang hymns. Nana didn't care.
I write this in the dark.
Their furniture is bolted in my rooms.
I cover it with cloth from Samarkand.

Now I sit atop green hair. The view is – coasts, fields and hills.
And I am still writing. My pencil in the sun.

This.

And if I carried not this saviour's dark, speech-figured,
tried inherit-house across the stones to This,
I might have written, climbing, or up here,
of beauty, place names, bees, formations,
midges, mist, islands, tides, yachts,
clouds, wind, forests, uncurling bracken,
fishing boats, clover, bluebells, seagulls, all,
as if they knew me more than His invention,
written, meant and moving, on the world.

Mad Mike: he's a motorbike manual!
by (Merv Read)/Read the Rock-Poet

Mad Mike: he's a motorbike manual!
Man he's so straight, he's almost mechanical.
Madness is just a frame of mind.
These days it's not so hard to find,
with his Wellington boots and his yellow leggings,
the kind you'd find outside the skins
of bananas he eats as he goes to tea.
Mad Mike are you so unhappy?
Mad Mike starts thinking!
Then he starts drinking
and fighting and sinking
into the world where his memory lives
where everything once was happy.
Now people are talking,
looking and walking
and wondering where Mike's gone.

Mad Mike: he's a motorbike manual!
Man he's no fool with his looks, has an animal's
broken red nose, something like a beak
and his glasses, they are perched on the peak.
When he does work, it's as if he's been hit
by a brick that's so thick you won't find the pit
that's as deep as the one where they dug the clay.
Mad Mike will you work today?
Mad Mike starts thinking!
Then he starts drinking
and fighting and sinking
into the world where his memory lives,
where everything once was happy.
Now people are talking,

looking and walking,
and wondering where Mike's gone.

Mad Mike - he's part of a library:
A, B, C, D, E, F and G.
Like an octave of sound
if left around,
it just fades awa-a-a-y!!!

Tower by John Watkins

Your strength is unity
Always was.
You took control
Bought out
Became a resistance.
People Power produced
A new Black Harvest.

The fruits of your labour
Became an inspiration to others
A blood red beacon
As the flag of 1831
Flew proud against injustice.

You leave black faces
Red tongues
In pages and photographs
We can all share
And tell the next generation.

The seams now exhausted.

Job done.

Birthday Lunch by Pip Smith

She watches me fumble the asparagus tongs
Not Like That she shows *Like This*
That's how the staff do it
Her words stretched taut like ballet hair
I turn to a new task and cut my hand on the corkscrew

My sister spinster daughter of the wrong mother
Places her grace as if freshly dusted on the mantle piece
And winces when siblings clutter the teak
With their bleeding hands *Stop crying*
She cuts through the mess

Underneath the lacework – French lace a delicate net –
A child swims cold spirals through her still gene pool
Or it's a mood she wears them like the ghosts of children lost
They cling round her middle round her neck She stands up
As I unwrap

She has bought too many presents and lets
The crackle of wrapping paper do the talking
She would have love constructed
But little does she know under her taut netting
Love gushes Wilder than it does in us

Now in this light she is still seven
Wanting her hair to be stroked
Her face to be turned into a warm belly
Wanting ribbons and new shoes and bakery smells!
Wanting Love in all its pink suffocation

And our mother who lines our speech our tastes our bones with
her genes

Our mother tells me later
She has no idea whose helix spun
That spinster sister of mine,
Because it certainly didn't come from her.

His Greatest Fear by Leah Armstead

sleeping late again

sleep that lies heavy
like a lion atop him
pressing what feels like
the last breath
out of him

windows closed

curtains drawn tight

it's dark enough to be night
but it's day

he'll win this fight

push off
run for the bus
get to work
and every hour
of waking
long for sleep
though it holds him
down and almost
won't release him

his greatest fear
is now
being awake

The Milky Way by Megan Vaughan

Silence
There is nothing to be heard
Everything is still
No laughter, no fun
Silence

Emptiness
There are no sides, just a plain black horizon
Leading to nowhere
No people, no life, no cause
It is empty

Darkness
A blanket of shadows, a hurtling wind
There is no way out
No one to lean on, no one to care
Darkness

No one
No one to talk to, no one is there
No one to live with, an endless stare
No one to cry with, no one to love
No land, no water, no reason to live

Silence, its is the sound of the Milky Way

The 2009 Winners
Judged by Mike Jenkins

the origami lesson by John Gallas

To make Derry Railway Station,
fold the gentle Foyle
beside this end, thus,
where the train breathes at a slight curve,
and for the white fence,
press the line
upon the middle crease
in a fine rain, then
unfold the sheeted roof wing by wing
in line with dim bridges
and the rounded wall.

For Evarethilion,
begin by folding lengthwise
and separating
amongst bright enamels.
To make the unearthly shine,
fold the top point –
which will be the blade –
into a garnet beast, and double back
the silver pommel
into the dotted fist.
Align the creases as if
a rainbow were a staircase
upon which
folded feet boldly tread.

The leaping gnu.
You may use the shimmer
from a lake amidst grassland,
but a hill will do.
Divide the top half into three hearts:

cow, horse and goat.
Take point X upon the hoof
and fold the top edge, thus,
upon its grunt,
so it is roughly equal
to the distance from
the far sun that pours
beneath black clouds to the brown,
dusty horizon.
To make the water,
turn the world over,
and crease.
Your gnu will fall from the mountain fold
towards sunset.
The valley fold will open upon it,
and his beautiful beard
will make a tasselled shadow.

Nan Follows the Bikers on a Day Out by Eluned Rees

Leather bodies burn past, squeezing
the life out of the valleys. Sleet
does for a blanket to cover a skinny
pony up by the monolith.
She's shouting as they drive past:
push that old thing over! A girl
rolls head over heels down the mountain,
squashes the terrace flat as a worm trail.

Past Ammanford, through Llanelli
they come to pine trees and dunes.
Nothing to hold onto but prickly
bog grass; sand sliding about, bits
of surf blowing like sheep's wool.

The sea goes quiet like a choir
lined up and all ready to sing.
A hang glider in the sky throws
a great shadow over the sea; Jonah's
whale is under the waves, gob wide.

A black bird struts on the beach,
beak like a knobbly nose, looking
over its shoulder, wanting them
to know it's special; a young thing,
or old and cross, its feathers all
sticking up. Then it's all wings
lifting off, swerving inland,
tipping off the flat edge
like young men's toes.

Ravens come with a warning,

she tells them. *You'll have to wait*
another bloody eighty years
to know what it is.

Rails by Lynn Roberts

From the platform's lip the railway lines
      don't promise well;

midden leavings trailing the station's length:
half a dead pigeon, cellophane from straws,
a matted lilac glove and Starbuck's cup;
wrappers and tissues, cans, a grubby doll,
receipts and tickets... Wooden sleepers gone
as shelves in Docklands flats; the scalloped edge
along the canopy gone too, with all those other things
you see on film – the fire buckets and brass,
the beds of flowers, the slow out-hiss of steam;
replaced by concrete slabs and henna stains
wept by the ironwork on the filler stones:
the rails don't promise well.

But the fine curl of the line under the
wishbone bridge gleams with promise; gleams, promising
meowing gulls over the promenade,
land folding out to sheep-specked ruckled hills,
Agatha Christie towns, huge airports, pristine, fresh;

runaway destinations, Eden clean;
no grey detritus, trailing rubbish, dirt;
no baggage of a complex grubby life;
no screwed-up Kleenex, sloughed-off feelings there;
only new gardens to re-root with flowers,
with trees whose promise is a genesis

before the serpent sways along the cut.

the origami lesson by John Gallas

The winning poem struck me immediately as a glorious 'leap' of the imagination (rather like the 'gnu' in verse three!). I admired greatly the notion of creating places and animals out of paper intricacies and the spare, instructional tone is wonderfully counter pointed by the glint of its language throughout. It moves so very subtly, verse by verse, from the mundane to the mythical and on to a conclusion which brings all the elements together in a gently universal manner without the need for any kind of grandiose statement. It recalled haiku both in content and style with its emphasis on the tactile and visual and with its vital purpose – 'No ideas but in things'.

Nan Follows the Bikers on a Day Out by Eluned Rees

The second prize-winner was so close I would've been tempted to award a joint first. Its comic title immediately grabbed me and there were certainly humorous touches elsewhere achieved through hyperbole, as the old woman follows the movement of the bikers. It's also a journey back into her past, bridged by the lines - 'A girl / rolls head over heels down the mountain... 'It is undoubtedly a filmic poem, whose movement is captured so well from valley down to shoreline and, in a final return, back to the Nan herself (who is akin to the black bird on the beach) and her last, sweeping statement. Like the winner, it has boldness of conception and isn't content to give a single perspective. Seamus Heaney, master of this, would admire such transformations.

Rails by Lynn Roberts

The third choice 'Rails' is a poem if initial stasis with an ever-roaming eye, evoking the minutiae of a station. The simple personification of 'platform's lip' works well, suggesting a journey, a word, a beginning. I liked especially the grubby grime of the descriptions, having spent many an hour at such places. It reminded me very much of Ponty station, with those 'henna stains'. Then, the movement in the poet's imagination brought out the stark contrasts between these rails and where they were leading: promenade, hills and airport (again Ponty is relevant). The Biblical imagery is introduced rather belatedly, but nevertheless proves effective, developing from 'Eden clean' to 'genesis' and finally the 'serpent', which strangely echoes the earlier 'out-hiss of steam'.

Mike Jenkins, August, 2009

Specially Commended, 2009

Shipbuilding by David Ford

My uncle Jim built ships,
not the real kind but *Airfix* kits,
twisting the plastic bits
free from their flimsy frame,
the skin skinning glue –
KEEP AWAY FROM FLAMES
- that would always stick
fingers into a permanent click
and form soft stalactites
on the end of the tube.

Enamelled red and white liners
sailed round the room,
fat bellied on grey hydrofoils:
one six hundred scale.
A *Humbrol* regatta
coasting the pelmets,
the drinks cabinet
and the radiogram.

Those were the days –
when the British merchant fleet
ruled the waves,
ploughing through surf doilies,
over a Pledge polished seas:
the Lusitania, the Lancastria,
the Mauritania
and RMS Britannic.

And in pride of place
in the middle of the sideboard,
the prow of the Titanic,

sailing with orchestra full blast
through a storm of plastic flowers,
towards a disaster of a table lamp.

Corposant by Gareth Roberts

Where the wind comes and the weed comes;
where the wrack and drift and wrecks come,
your boots stumble
on empty mussels
to bruise dull purples
on the storm's edge. A ragged man:

again you come to disturb slits
that once were mountains. In your fists
is the grasp of grit
to unthread holes in pockets
and lose things more precious
to the sand. You stand

your sodden, unlit beacon that does not beckon
and does not burn away the rime
on your boots: salted epithets,
lost and writ again
while the ship-wrecks come and go.
The sea has cured you; a dried branch

that will not bend and will not sink but is tossed,
forever, to this naked stretch. Your eyes,
like broken mussels,
wait for crabs.
And all about is the ragged edge
of close and closed horizons.

      Here

               breakers are sighing in the weed;

      here

winds run whistling through dune-grass.

If you close your battened eyes you can hear the
music
of faraway songs by faraway, smothered lamps
where peat fires tempt toes to tingle and knit
the thread of old flames. And somewhere,

beyond the sea, the herring are still singing:
somewhere, behind the clouds, St Elmo's fire is
wringing ichor
from the storm; somewhere, beneath the waves,
the selkie waits.

Wasted by Gareth Roberts

There were nights dancing so bright
with the half laugh
and your eyes hurt. You were smoke
and I breathed you deep until the white lights came.

Barefoot on the street with broken glass
we ran, and made our faces strange
in taxi-backs and bus-backs
and railway tracks: hand-rolled.
Every day was a blister that we popped;
us, the torn skin, the scab roughed off;
the slow, limping weed on rocks at low-tide: gasping;
waiting for Gauguin or Dali
or a simple impress on the sand
with our toes and our hair.

When the pier burned we were there,
slow-walking, hand in hand;
and the band played
through the storm of sparks
and blistered Victoriana;
and I danced
while you burned.

I remember smoke;
the taste of smoke,
the sting, the smarts,
the tarts or smoke:

your face
disappearing.

When she was very young by Rebecca Carrington

take a sultry breeze,
wrap it like a scarf
round her shoulders,

take twenty grey-brown
pebbles that she found
and wanted to keep
in your pocket,

take the sand,
sculpt for an hour
into Eeyore, then
wonder at her glee
as she kicks him down,

take her splashes, take her slips
among rocks, take her tears,
kiss barnacle-bitten hands better,

take her home,
but bring her back
again and again.

Wasp... by David Butler

...leaves its paper-lantern nest,
a painted samurai.

September has filled it
with the jitters.
When it crawls the globe
of a pitted wind-fall
wings fidget
to right its stumbling.

Its antennae are
nerve ends.

A humour
of the grey air
has maddened the venom
inside its double-
jointed abdomen;
black-bile;
yellow-bile.

It can sense the end.

Now it turns
kamikaze:
launching
into one last
delirious flight
it is
fanatic,
frenetic,
simply dying

to fall upon the sword.

Luna by Ben Ziman-Bright

Last night, because I wanted to show you
that I would give you the moon if I could,
I stole it. Nobody noticed
and, by the time it was back in my room,
I had got away with the whole thing.

It wasn't enough.
I wanted you to know
that even the moon meant less,
so I spent last night
smoothing out each crater
and painting your portrait
in the moon-dust.

When I replaced it just before dawn,
the absence was noted
and there were consequences.
My name was in the paper,
on the BBC, and even
the President of the Royal Astronomical Society
wrote me a strongly-worded letter
condemning what I had done.

But later, as he watched the moonlight
pool and settle soundlessly
on his bed's once-warm other side,
he telephoned
to say he understood why I had done it.

Pins by Graham Burchell

Sharp things together scratch
at the imprint of early learning.

Never test a blade with a finger or play
with wood with sticking out nails.

Do not poke knitting needles or folded tapers
of silver paper at the glow of an electric fire.

Do not kiss slugs, nettles or the necks of roses.
Do not eat worms, abide spiders

or waggle canes in wasps' nests
because only people accept apologies.

Put the pricking and thin-stemmed,
thin-legged things next to each other;
among them, potential perpetrators
of cruel incursions into other bodies.

Impale flies on pins embedded
in cork next to a cork speared with blackthorns
above other thorns and a small wishbone.

Display them like mantelpiece pistols,
but on Tom Thumb shelves of aluminium
juxtaposed with holly, the hard boy of leaves.
Spear one twice. Stick it with wood!

Stick a berry, a pinecone and an acorn.
Make stabbing a thing of beauty.
Introduce a tiny flower. Violate

its coiled paper capitulum
with brass petals of chopped up staples.

Metal things, like pins (safety, hat, hair)
and varied lengths and points of nail
speak as nature shouts –

back off, or we'll come in. Crucify!

("Pins" Found objects and mixed media by Fionna Hesketh)

Buzzards over Fleam Dyke by Harry Goode

Fancy seeing you here! Of all places!
I know, of late, you've travelled far from home,
away from *cwms* where cling the stunted oaks,
from *frydds* that flank the *mynydd*'s wind-scraped heights.

One time I saw thirty or more of you,
sailing over Kinsley in bright spring air,
sated on rabbit flesh, seeking a mate
to build, ramshackle sticks, the season's nests.

I should have known that you would end up here.
I heard you crying in the city streets
at Oxford, why only this summer past,
sounding plaintive, as though you mourned the hills.

Your black neighbours have yet to learn your ways,
have yet to learn the need to drive you off.
Briefly you may flaunt on Fleam Dyke's scant rise,
a lordly looking, hungry, beggared bird.

One more to work the Oliver Hammer 1899 by Silvia Millward

What kind of mother am I
when I cannot stop to clean my children?
Sweat trickles down my face,
then falls, hissing, on the red hot metal.
Sparks fly from my hammer
as I join link into link,
blister on my long-numb hand.

My man works hard
taking only three pence
for a quart of beer;
he will sleep
all the heavier for drink,
while I hide my secret
beneath a ragged nightdress.

Head upon straw pillow,
I envy those hammers hitting anvils
sounding out through the night,
as younger and stronger women than I
make heavier chains
that will put good food on the table,
as I once did.

Tomorrow morning my eldest
will work the bellows,
as sickness consumes me.
She is a child still,
often falling asleep
as we work,
and I regretfully nudge awake.
My flyaway hair,

tight within metal curlers,
will be combed out on Sunday,
when I look at myself
and see my grandmother's
determined chin
and my mother's wrinkled brow.

A thick leather apron
protects my body,
bellows at my side,
hand clutching hammer.
I have worked like this
since before my marriage bed
and when I carried my babies.

Nursed, weaned
and rocked to the chime
of the Oliver Hammer
my children dream
of nothing more
than enough bacon and potatoes
to feed us all.

A walk with God by Patricia Bellotti

God said, Take Me for a walk
somewhere you have never been. Great,
I said, I'll make a picnic, loaves and fishes –
tuna mayo actually – and He said that was OK.
then I asked Him if He spoke Welsh because
He would have to say Afon Llwchwr
to everyone when He got home.

We started at the river's eye where
the water springs in spurts. Isn't it lovely
I asked Him, paddling your toes? We came
to a feeder-stream whose name I forget
and my river grew stronger. Listen,
it's singing, I said, and God smiled,
hummed along with it.

Now look here, I said, this is where
the fun begins. I've seen it on the OS map;
twists and bends, puddles and ponds,
it'll take us all day to reach the river's end.
I'll carry you, God said, jump up on My back.

And on His shoulder I fell asleep, fell
back into my dream of the river,
the place where I have never been.

Easter Monday by Isobel Norris

That Easter, walking miles of sanded bay,
we split our kisses ever smaller, thaws
across our frosted skin. We only paused
to see the sky turn red from hours of grey,
to eat the satsumas and clementines
we bought the day before in Sainsbury's.
The sun was fading fast behind the trees;
we kissed in glowing dusk, forgot the time.

Do you remember afterwards, we woke
too warm, too late, and vaguely lost; to sheets
that stung of gone-off fruit? Our mouths
were citrus raw, the air was screaming sweet
with spoiling mandarins and tangerines
that peeled, uncurled, like ashes in the heat.

The Gatekeeper by Deborah Harvey

There's no one left to mourn them.
Only stony-faced angels keep watch
over the names of forgotten children,
written in lichen,
blotted with moss.

Flowers must bring themselves:
dandelions for Mary Kate;
stately cuckoo-pints for Diana,
the siren shine of malevolent berries
no longer a worry.

From the tower
the clock strikes four quarters and one.
A gatekeeper settles on a stone.
Its wings wear the colours of autumn fallen,
umber and rust.

A clatter of jackdaws comes bustling back,
tatters the death pall with tender talk.
Playground voices shoulder through oak trees,
boisterously singing
the Hokey-Cokey.

First Baron Cawdor of Castlemartin by Emily Hinshelwood

God knows how you bribed your peerage.
Services to Pitt? Or was it chocolate house
chat that got you sat to squat on this bit
of cracked ocean? If we're talking lines,
Stackpole's a fair whack from your castle.

So, you dug lily ponds, hollowed a quay
juxtaposed genteel lakes with the hammering
sea. Gazed on pink petals when all around
the price of barley was just out of reach.

But nothing wears out a fine face like democracy.
Lilies still outgrow Lords;
they open flowers to damselflies
as the world shifts in the sky.

Court is toppled to stones; threadbare coat
of arms hangs dusty; crinolined ladies
in Barafundle Bay – all just sand to the warren.
And Stackpole Quay? It's full of chocolate house chat
and Green & Blacks and pots of fair-trade tea.

Finding the Darkness by James Knox Whittet
(Sestina For Wittgenstein In Connemara)

*I can only think clearly in the dark and in Connemara I have found one of
the last pools of darkness in Europe*

I see you standing alone in darkness
in that garden hedged with wet fuchsias,
listening intently to the strange language
of seabirds who ghost above Atlantic waves;
broken sentences of staccato lights
from the skerry interrupting your thoughts.

Often, spectres of death would stalk your thoughts
like fluttering storm petrels in darkness,
their deep set eyes pinpricked with lights.
Breezes would shake stamens of fuchsias,
pebbled shores would be shoved aside by waves
of the vast sea's bewildering language.

In the *Tractatus*, you opened language
to make a window for the world of thoughts
but the Irish tongue surged in spuming waves,
dancing in reels of their verbal darkness
as pearls of rain balanced on fuchsias
and the sky was ribboned with shafts of lights.

From the eyes of cottages, all the lights
have gone; you imagine the lost language
of famished men who lay beneath fuchsias
in storms, dead children ghosting through their thoughts.
Where is God, to whom you prayed, in darkness?
You listen to silences between waves.
Each day, you watch gannets explode in waves;

111

cormorants hang their wings in shifting lights
when watered sun folds back sheets of darkness
from this land which is woven in language:
each field, pool, rock, are named, where words and thoughts
are layered like turf, brushed by fuchsias.

The stilled air is heavy with fuchsias'
honeyed scent, midges rise as one in waves
from soaked moss; clarity enters your thoughts
like sudden arrow showers tipped with lights;
luminous as scoured landscape and language
in sudden revelations of darkness.

Above high fuchsias, you glimpse strange lights
that fall in waves, unsayable language
beyond thoughts: you reach to embrace darkness.

lights in water by John Gallas

I zip my coat and watch the reservoir
go blue. It's cold tonight. Then grey. Then black.
Behind a nubbled spiny hedgerow cars
shine on and off along its sodium track –
streetlamp – streetlamp – streetlamp... Clouds are lying.
I watch, open-mouthed. These lines of light,
unmirrored till the water, draw and dip and –
streetlamp – streetlamp – streetlamp – suddenly stand,
like alcazarous pillars, liquid-bright,
under the water-brim. I sand up crying.

Down there is Faeryland: a swimming,
lambent city built with yellow light.
This lustred dream fills my eyes, brimming
at some belief. And more: through the night,
paddling over all this gleam-piled trick,
come two white swans, more picture-poems than things,
to get me. Should I go? Black-borne bubbles
silver-slip: the world is full of troubles –
pillar – pillar – pillar – Something sings.
Laughter. They are passing. Moon-bells. Quick.

I splash along the low-hedge, glow-edge track.
The swans bob and wait. The clouds still lie.
I reach my foot to one white basket-back...
As if I could. What feather-prince am I
to tread on dreams? Streetlamp – streetlamp – streetlamp –
The swans cut away. The music dies.
Behind the hedges cars shine on and off.
I put my drizzled hood up, shiver, cough,
and find my car-keys, sniff and wipe my eyes,
all runny with the dam-deceitful damp.

Head Case by Phil Knight

The Monday after Blair Peach a teacher
and Anti-Nazi League member was killed
on a demo by a Special Control Group baton.
We were filing into line for

Metal Work the first lesson of
the week, when one of the boys
started to softly sing something
so the rest of us craned forward

in order to catch his almost
silent words but his rasping voice grew
in resonance and its strength and
joy filled the corridor.

"Oh The White Man's Front
is the National Front,
So join the National Front".
He repeated this mantra over and

over again and when the class
backed off he began a wild rioting dance
part Saturday Night Fever
part Storm Trooper.

The Metal Work room door clanged open
and Dai Spanner our teacher bellowed,
"YOU BOY HEAD MASTER",
He was white hot with anger.

Mr Spanner grabbed the offender by
his collar and he was frog marched

away to an encounter with the dreaded
School Leader.

We never saw much of him after that.

Two decades later I met him
by chance in a petrol station
he was well turned out in a new grey suit
white shirt and red tie.

His hair was brushed forwards
in a vain attempt to hide a large black
Swastika tattoo which had pride of place
in the centre of his forehead.

He said he was off to a job
interview but was not hopeful,
there was "bugger all work out there".
I did not venture an opinion why.

The day I ate what I thought was a magic mushroom
by Leah Armstead

I'd heard that magic mushrooms grow in cow fields
and can make you see God and angels that really glow,
so on the annual Church Youth Retreat into the wilderness
I brought along a Guide to Mushrooms and wandered off
at the first chance I could, wandering until I heard the lowing
of cows, and spotted what seemed the mushroom of my dreams.
I was very scared, but it was sacred somehow, and I chewed the
 thing
carefully like a Communion wafer. It tasted like snail dust and
 worms.
I laid back on the grass for a few hours, as if taking in the summer
 sun.
Nothing happened. Really frightened now, I trod back to the camp
slipping into a Prayer Meeting as inconspicuously as I could.
A girl I know to be a goody-goody-two-shoes was crying out to God
about all of her sins. Well, if she had sins, what did I have?
I was about to die an unforgivable death. I'd checked the book
and there was one fungi that looked a lot like a magic mushroom
but was deadly and would kill you very painfully in about 12 hrs.
Since I wasn't conversing with any angels
I figured I'd eaten the lethal one and had about 9 hours left.

I waited for the horrible pains. The prayer meetings went on.
I didn't eat my dinner because I'd soon be vomiting uncontrollably.
Maybe I'd be one to skip the pains and just suddenly die in the night.
Singing round the camp-fire tears streamed down my hell-red
 cheeks.

Everyone just thought I was very touched by the Holy Spirit
and hugged me hard and said "God loves you and so do I!"
Who would have thought I'd die surrounded by happy, hollering

Holy Roller teenagers? I'd only recently become a teenager myself.
And now look what was happening, I'd soon be dead, so young.
I took it in some stride. My lips were sealed, I couldn't speak.
There was no antidote, the book said. What would be, would be.

In my cot that night I found breathing a task too much, and my
    heartbeat
broke the sound barrier. The girls in my cabin slept on, clean of
    conscience.
I cried silently, missing my family, upset that I would be disgraced,
dying – at a church retreat, no less – like some desperate druggie,
all because I was trying to get high enough to see God!

Well, that much was coming true. I'd soon see God face-to-face
as he sadly announced that due to unpardonable sin, I was Satan's
    own.
If hell it was to be, then hell it would be. It was too late now.
My tears dried up. It was over. It was done. And I fell asleep.

When I woke, I was still in one piece on my cot in the cabin
in a woods with wild birds singing in spirited tongues to the
    heavens.
Was it possible? That ugly little mushroom wasn't lethal after all!
Or maybe it had been a miracle? It didn't matter any more.
Angels and magic disappeared into scrambled eggs, forever.

The 2010 Winners
Judged by John Evans

Litzmannstadt 1941 by Sally Spedding

Each day she'd wondered who lived in that slab of a
house; climbed its stairs to hot attic rooms beneath
the reddest tiles of all, slipped a little over the years,
but still a roof she loved.
Who owned next door, grey and green, which Emilie
Floge opined was too dark, out of keeping with the
huddle of dwellings corralled between water and the
place of prayer...
Safer than Purkersdorf. Safer than here...

When they press a black spoon to her lips and say
"eat," she does. When they tear the fur and her dress from
her back, force her to stand like a dead, bare tree
she says, "feel free."
When they hack at her hair and the pieces fall like the
years of her life, freezing her scalp, brushing both
knees, she's Emilie, not Amelia clasping that sturdy arm
as they move through the stillness away from the lake
with the sun on their faces. God in their hearts...

"There'll be no shadows, no black-tongued Leyladii, no
man nor beast, no inkling of evil, just a bright holiness,"
is his promise. And then come bells – *Angelus domini
nuntiavit Mariae* – uno, due, tre, quattro...
The Church at Cassone re-born...

"Boiled mouse or barley beans? Water or piss? Take your
pick." But her voice is still, her stomach shrunk while
lice grow fat and the star on her breast has turned to stone;
while that slab of a house and its curious peace, those hot attic
rooms and roof so red, are beckoning, waiting

Purkersdorf – a Viennese suburb where the Zuckerlandl's home – The Westend Sanatorium passed to Viktor's sister Amelia. When she was sent to the Lodz ghetto (Litzmannstadt) in 1941, Klimt's painting of 'The Church at Cassone' that she'd so carefully hidden, was looted by the Nazis.

Izzy by Nigel Ormond

Burbling stream
Wooden bridge, fallen tree
Which I sat on
And had a smoke
With Izzy.

Go with Otto now
Wooden bridge has gone
Stopped smoking
A year ago, and
Izzy's gone. Not far,
In the back garden
Actually, in between the
Bay windows. South facing
Sunny and warm
She felt the cold but
She doesn't need her
Red coat, not now
Or ever.

She walked
Or swaggered really in a
Very feminine, canine way
Tail wagging, tongue overhanging
Eyes smiling, always pleased to see
Anyone, anytime, anywhere.

Uninitiated people, can't help it,
Thought she was a cross- a cross
Dalmatian. You see she was iced
White, cool as a cucumber with
Black spots, not mouldy. She was very definitely

Pure Whippet. Who's ever seen
Dalmatian's with shapely quarters,
Steep underline, deep
Depth of brisket, I ask you. Leave
A Dalmatian on the blocks. Nice
Dogs but not a frigging Whippet
Look alike! Nothing like.

Good lungs, shit off a shovel,
Swimming with Dolphins,
Swimming with Whippets,
Plucky little girl, but at least
When it happened she was in full
Flight, oblivious, enjoying life
Until death. A few years
Premature, but, she used
Her 8 years, full throttle
Full on, in your face in
A nice way
Rest her soul.

Waiting by Jane Fox

In a moment vast landscape of tolerance tired sore love
Sunlight dusk light dark light sweet complicity
Still here
First bell lush leaves crackling wind waving
Darker lighter hues snap snap
Lacy skeletal love
Heart solitary white bell
Furry flight dandelion perpendicular stern stem darkened golden
   threads sun on face
Awaiting sweetheart luminescent antennae
Smell fresh greens like fresh greens
Two headed white flanks daisy smothered hot snow
Marbled stained mud grades curtained chomping bones tendons
   beneath
tongue gyrating swallows hind back to earth cycling air ride me ride
   me
large irritation nettled lengths grey trunks eager hunger stung
   poisoned
liquor and the Neptunian stubborn proud unyielding hover paler
   redder
greener blacker docks long strain squeaked heart ravaged like an old
   rag
Spiney prong lush fern vessel curling limbs embrace bell swamp
Loneliness of the wait labyrinthine bowels
Crying of the lost black belly where light bereft bloated
   love-mirrored spectre
Killing of the wait
Red trampled chambers pulsating refusal
Come out into the light disembodied single note
Waiting
Never don't ever Always all this time So long still Holding and
   Holding

Holding
Will not without possibility consideration
Till dark elusive resurgent refusal torment straining remains
Not of it
To be
Consumed insidious optimism usurped realigned functionless
    essence of
    this
Here
Swallowed
Assimilated
Blinded
Still here Still Waking You Uppermost Left For another Still love you
Never expected Still Love you
Want you Long To see you Do you think of me Do you
How much longer will I love you Cannot One love
Wish you could If only You could
Love
Continue Hunger constant hunger Continue
Alone Solace Wither skeletal leaf Dancing Without Sweet unyielding
    lover
Look to the time it stops Knowing it won't
The difference is as much as I love you
You've lost And freed me
To love
Continue
Take another step Slowly move away
Still

Litzmannstadt 1941, by Sally Spedding

Excellently written. A narrative poem whose shifts and turns propel the reader through an episode in one of humankind's darkest eras. The "story" is complex – even if you know just some of the history of those involved. Klimt, his lover Emilie Klöge, and his painting, Church in Cassone. Viktor Zuckerkandl, the owner of the painting until it passed into the hands of his sister, Amelie Redlich, who tried to hide the painting from the Nazi's, before she was deported to Lodz in Poland and never seen again. No matter how compelling, how emotive, how shocking a subject, no historical account of dates facts and figures can ever come close to portraying that personal immediacy, that insight into the complexity of human experience, but a poem can make us imagine, and a great poem, such as this, can bring us very close indeed. "When they tear the fur and her dress from / her back, force her to stand like a dead, bare tree / he says, "feel free." Not that you need to know the story to appreciate and be moved by this poem. No dry prose, this. Lyrical, emotional, inventive, and bursting with imagery. "There'll be no shadows, no black-tongued Leyladii, no". Technically accomplished. Verse to give voice to the unspeakable. A very worthy winner.

Izzy, by Nigel Ormond

The art and craft of writing good poetry is to make it look easy, to make the writer invisible, in order that the subject matter, imagery, and musical qualities are allowed to shine through. But, behind the apparent simplicity and ease this poem is written with great skill and technical ability. Word play, wit, unexpectedness of thought, depth of feeling, musical, vivid images – honed, and finely chiselled to the absolute essentials, not a word wasted. Enjambment, caesura, and end stopped lines take us back and fore in time on a journey that touches us. "Izzy's gone. Not far, / in the back garden / Actually, in between the / Bay windows." Happy, sad, and at times funny, but all of the time very, very moving. "She felt the cold but / She doesn't need her / Red coat, not now / Or ever." No cold stone memorial, this is a living breathing (barking) celebration of life in all it's complexity. A poem about a dog, about someone who owned and loved a dog, about a dog who loved it's owner; a poem about love, and life and loss; a poem about all of us, about all of our lives. Great poems make the personal into the universal. This poem does just that, a worthy prize winner in any poetry competition.

Waiting, by Jane Fox

This poem is a symphony of words, tones and colours. "In a moment vast landscape...". A language poem. A dance with words. Words being used as language rather than rhetoric. Words for words sake. Art for arts sake. Part chant, part spell and incantation, the natural imagery drawing language back to it's more primitive and visceral origins. "Marbled stained mud grades curtained chomping bones tendons...". You don't need to "get it". The poem drifts in and out of meaning; that poetic space between sense and non sense where true thought and emotion exist without constraint. New syntactic relationships emerge. Sometimes the combinations of unexpected words create a sensation of newly created, forever permutating sense, "squeaked heart ravaged like an old rag". The writer pays careful attention to the musical qualities of the poem – the rhythmic weight, the alliterative connections, the sound, tone and texture. A fragmented narrative appears here and there, somewhere just under the surface, "Still here Still Waking", until, at the last gasp a voice emerges for a moment, "You've lost And freed me / To love / Continue". Inventive, challenging and very well written.

John Evans, July 2010

Specially Commended, 2010

Jetsam by Noel Williams

Fingering steel, under grey Nikes
slung on the phone wire, nogo,
she hooks him, her tail sea-slick,
wrapped in wave-wrack and salt.
He drops the half-brick, hearing the fornicating sea.
She is red, blue, red, pea-green, red
in the off-on of money machines.
It's the spill of coins scraping
as he enters her, potting her, holing her.
It's the headless thrush buckled in the drain
that flickers green, red, as he stubs himself on her.
But she shrugs her skirt, clips his beak, stops
breathing. He spreads his hand against the shop window crack,
its snap the sound of shipwreck.
Her pimp unspools a wire.
The carotid of the street seeps
to the sound of the stopped clock over the boathouse.
Tide sucks and sucks the last mound of sand.

Polly by Ashley Bovan

Damn lambs,
ratty,
dressed in flem,
fluff,
weather in sky,
wiggly piglets grub in sties
on banks of stream
where fallen trees rest and rot,
bugs bug, sing to calves
and surprise! Hey! Donkeys!
Ice lolly, tacky, red chem. stain
sticks ants to chin,
clouds, like painting,
path, like map,
water very cold today,
dog with muck stuck on fur
shakes eyes and teeth with gummy grin,
rattle of leash, buckles and clips,
wave my arm, chop the air,
do kung fu,
do not tread in dog pooh,
boat putt putts past birds that fight
and cheep and eat, scraggy, stupid,
fast, so fast, zip here, zoom there,
flit through fences, bushes, logs,
books stacked beside the fire,
covers, granules of disease,
tired, chair, glass of wine,
toasty feet and there's a dog
I must have got
earlier
when I was out walking.

A pen portrait of my ex-lover by Penny James

He is an empty biscuit barrel,
A chipped wine glass,
Litres of cider
And late night movies.

He is a week of nightmares,
Packs of sleeping tablets,
A mathematical formula
And the last piece of cheesecake.

He is 6 o'clock Saturday morning starts,
He is windy wide open spaces,
Greenness and golf clubs.
He is watching snooker and cricket on telly,
Cigarettes and chocolate bars,
An open box of condoms on the dressing table,
A snazzy low-slung purple car and wet shaves.

He is wraparound sunglasses,
Soaking up the rays
And tiny, lime green swimming trunks.

He is James Dean cool
Because he knows no better,
He is a wasteland
Leading on to urban familiarity,
Rural fertility
And suburban conformity with confusion
That shapes and marks him,
Beneath the skin, unseen graffiti;
The forgotten architecture of his soul,
An outpouring of unhappiness.

He is The Pogues, Nick Cave and The Stereophonics,
A non-dancer, out of reach, almost present, casual and banal.
He is toasted cheese sandwiches
And The Independent newspaper.
He is BBC News 24
A denim jacket, striped pyjamas,
Navy blue Primark pants
And a silver cigarette-rolling machine.
This is his dream machine
When filled with Golden Virginia.

Shifts by Pat Borthwick

Night roads are thick with hitchhikers.

Once, not long off the ferry at Caen,
my full-beam stared into bandit eyes,
two polecats on hind legs peering
from the verge through bracken.
I've been hostage to them since.

Another time, a trembling deer,
its ears scooped forward to my engine,
legs flickering like altar candles.

I pull over in the lay-by
to step out of speed, check my map.
Bats darken gaps between the stars.
I could be bound up in this solid knot
except my torch illuminates
their fleet separateness. I switch off

and dark fuses us together
in one witch-black swirl.

I love these luminal hours when a dim
hedge might twitch, a white-tipped tail
slip through, or a silver spray of wings
ghost across the windscreen. My car
records miles, my average speed.
An amber snowflake warns of ice.

I trust these backlit facts. Yet am I sure
my lifts don't know they ride with me
while still remaining where we met?

Still by Sue Lovell

I don't do much. I am
Mostly defined by what I am not.
Not the dead-eyed drone driving to a dull job, shackled by debt and
despair;
Not the frightening beauty, member of the girlie gaggle with the
killer giggle,
Skip-hopping in street synchronicity,
(At whom I gaze in fascination and feel, still, should be my friends).
Not the shiny-faced barmaid with red blotched skin - fat map of blue
tattoo and rope vein arms, yellow mouthed, laughing for a living;
Not the raggedy magazine seller hunched on the blanky, with the
dog-eared doggy, staring at the dirty;
Not the music-car punk, vibrating the air, fists gripped on wheel,
assenting to the rhythm in his moving metallic-trance-fizz of sound.

Neither baby-mother nor child any more,
Orphaned by time.
My descrying eye itself not seen.

I am not the kneeling gardener pulling dead primroses, forking the
sodden soil, wet wires of hair face-pasted by rain
And not the hundred shoes that I watch walking,
(because I look, always, down - it's the way my face faces.)

Not stupid.
Not the smiley, beardy, brain-injured tricycling man with shopping
basket balanced on the bars,
holding up the traffic, unignorable.
Nor the big blond lad named Brian, down our street, too large, too
old to play with the little kids but still liking to,
With his oriental almond eyes and numb, blubbery tongue.

Not I.
I know what I have become.

I am the shop-window ghost, grey, smudged.
I am the bus stop wraith, the fiddly change-purse in the charity shop.
I am the walking frame with wheels.
I am the senna pod joke, I am varicose, I creak
like an open door to an empty room.
I am transparent, mostly silent.
I do not make a fuss.

I am still.

Here.

Mr Selvridge Sketches by Richard Halperin

'At the Last Supper, they ate mackerels,'
said Mr Selvridge, and who could deny it?
Every day at the shore sketching. 'Thinnest
man I've ever seen,' said Mrs Barnes, 'and
the tallest.' 'Thinnest yes, tall no, short rather.'
(That was Mrs White, Ethna.) 'Isn't. 'Is.'
'Isn't.' 'Is.' A box of paints, a kind of easel,
the wind, Mr Selvridge. Pants. Shirt. That Hat.
Scarf. Every day. Even in winter, never
A coat. 'Turner sketched, I sketch. Turner
hadn't the Irish Sea. So there's room.'
Yellow daubs, green, one boat, two. A derrick
split maybe, a hand possibly, a foot
surely, but where? On the derrick. If a
derrick. Well, something pink, anyway. 'No
trigonometry, no towns,' he used to say.
'What's a town?' the tiniest girl you ever
saw asked. 'Right question,' he said. He was
the gentleman in the parlour, Hazlitt,
Maugham, that kind of person. Tidy room, read
by the fire, nice to talk to, missed his dog,
you could tell. Yellow daubs, green. The sun sets
in the east off the Irish Sea, thought he
said that. Not sure. So, no inverted commas.
Anyway, there's it on my wall, signed 'S,'
setting over Snowdonia. 'One day
I'll go to Wales,' he said. But he didn't.
Here's something exact: 'There are no good paintings,
only light and good puns of it. Fish are
silver, so they're not possible. That's why—
listen and learn—that's why I show I always
show the sea dazzle not from the sun over

but from the fish under. Look and learn.'
This to the Esterhazy boy, the one
who ate crayons only if they were ochre.
'Lovely difficult colour, ochre. Good lad.'
It was the last sketch got him. 'This one did me,'
he said to me. Or was it 'This one did *me*'?
The wind blew the words every way which.
We haven't seen him since. The sketch could have
a scarecrow in it. Could. Couldn't. Oh, I
forgot. 'Why'd you say "Listen" the first time?'
the Esterhazy boy'd asked. 'Did I?' said
Mr Selvridge. 'That's interesting.'

Llandudno by Helen Johnson

Held between the two arms
of the Great and Little Orme
the sea is steadied,
calm this morning.

Sun warms and dries
this strip of sand,
laid like a towel
at the foot of the town.

In the shelter, one man
with a banjo plays a tune
and each note is its own fine grain
set precisely in a line.

This morning I swim
in the polish and shine
of faded grand hotels,
in music clean as minnows,
in the lichen-gold of mirrors,
in the lull between two storms.

When you know the party's over before it's over by J. S. Watts

July comes quickly round again.
Half a year evaporates and what's to show?
No longed for dazzle that's for sure.
This, a year of living lightly
On the surface tension of my life,
Of dancing flighty glitter-ball dreams,
Twelve dragonfly months of rainbow skinned bubbles,
But the froth went flat
From a surfeit of mediocre
And the crystal it gushed from cracked
With six months left to go.
I'm dancing with flat feet from here on in,
But I never was Nureyev, no Fontaine;
An ugly duckling quacking the swan's swansong.
If the stage was empty
I'd not be asked to dance.
Yet I go on in the chipped belief
That perseverance conquers all,
Except maybe blisters;
A tortoise in sequinned tennis shoes
Still waiting for her invite.
The streamers, having fallen down, lie flat
Like last night's noodle takeaway.
Torn tinsel rustles in the sticky shadows
Looking for misplaced fantasies.
Someone will have to clear this mess
Before New Year.
Six months of shovelling dust.

Cynical Saviour? (maybe) by John Lusardi

I MMmmmmm sssssssssiiiiickkkkk of it, every *fucking* day,
                    Especially everyfffffufuuuckkkin morning
Mixed in with my weetabix, fruit and milk, I stir in, and spit out the
BBC,
  And that insipid grin phelgms to the floor – here we go again,
where the
                    feck is the button box?
                    Whoooooooowooo its -

1,500 tons of poisonous concrete multiplied by 22 times the original
amount gives us warmth,   Yeh,   Yeh!   and –
Saves the planet, that's already dead in the water,
We watch it spinning clockwise drain-bound and
  What about – the,
Millennium bug belief, Ha, Ha, and starving children fed, (cynic)
who?
In my head, Itssssssss all steam, piss and,   bullshit plated-to save
saviours

Oh go on – tell me again. Stop taking the piss!
Save money – it's meant for spending
Save life --- less of us – less carbon
Save lives --- as above
Save --- the planet – why?
Save time ---is it drowning in the egg timer sand?
Save souls – yours or mine?
Save you --- sod you
Save me – I'm the boss
Save us --- me first
Save coins – erase the queen's head! its history,
Save stamps – close a post office
Save fuel – burn chip fat, smell like a cod, don't catch one!

Save energy – turn on a light you won't bump into things!
Save tyres – where has all the rubber gone off worn tyres?
Save face – two-faced bastard
Save water – don't bath, save germs
Save food – eat shit or smoke it!
Save space – don't queue,
Save the word save, it may come in handy later on.
Mmmmm?
That's about it really, we need saving.

                                                            From ourselves?

When? – Yesterday!

Different by Jo Walters

The boys
Saw a white black-bird.

There he sat –
Improbable as a unicorn
Solid as a potato
Real as love –

Singing.

Because he was different
The boys
Grew very excited.

Because he was different
The boys
Stoned him to death.

Going Back by Terry Jones

i
A stretch of fence is fallen
where Commission land begins.
There are two old ewes there,
loitering in the long grass:
waiting like the dog on the whistle
they'll scamper up here to the gate,
puzzled, thistled, checking behind them.
You're stood in the barn's shadow
hand on the dog's black head,
looking with your father's eyes
straight down the field to Crookmullin.

ii
You bend to stoke a fox cub
scruffed out from the earth,
vixen dead on a snarl in heather.
Arthur brought it down from the forest,
balanced it on the shitty cobbles
to mewl and whisker in the yard;
bracken haunted, on its first legs,
the dogs want to kill it.
You look into its old eyes
with a child's belief in co-existence

iii
Now you're unborn.
Dad's with the team on Top Field,
those great horses that go one step at a time,
this step and that one
solving the puzzle of movement.
As moons of hooves rise and fall

he looks from under his cap:
house hangs on a rein of smoke
tying earth and evening.
Before he comes home she greets you
with a hand on her belly.

iv
Back yard ended where forest began:
you could go almost one step
from kitchen to bole and shadow,
straight to green darkness;
trees leaned at every window,
a nest against the glass upstairs.
But this is going back,
a time before you were conceived:
there was a road here then
that ended suddenly in the middle of the field.

the 2154 of this land by Steve Garside

Dusk mugs out the drowsing day,
a shopkeeper winks, a dog walker thinks,
a sniper-faced driver scowls about drinking.

Hope for the lost is primed with murmurs here
from the depths of a canal lock dredged -
the snug bones of fascination found slung
into boats filled with the already dead.

Headlights scream out for the hills,
as the evening is defeated by night,
words in shadows scuffle and kebab meat spits;
in the darkness, something cackles at life.

A Weekend on the Coast by Meghan Tally

Christopher sleeps and the day
feels full, the shortbread eaten,
paper mostly read. It is morning

where my past lives, afternoon
where I am, which has me
considering how white or late

the light, how green the water
at its cliffs. My hair goes red
in the afternoon, his mouth

a quicker mauve. We are young
but not as young as once we
were. Our sisters both bloom

again with child, and we await
the arrival like grandparents,
wanting only safe passage.

This wedge of years comes; we
look straight on, the country-
side before us, all the wind just
a comfort now. We are brave.

Estuary by Gareth Roberts

They have turned the mudflats into a marina:

where wading-birds stalked the silts for their treasures,
lost beneath water-sports and un-sailored yachts
tethered to "THE OYSTERCATCHER".

      On the seafront
      an artist has made something clever
      from an anchor.

They have squashed that which could not be squashed,
stopped the waves that turned back the ships and the coal.

           We sold our homes for a hole in the green-slide
valley,

      our lungs for dust; our loved ones
      for a fair wind and sails
      with old songs
      for a new world.

      Trees
      from the felled land
      creak
      on the waves.

           The farmer tips his axe to wood, his plough
    to earth;
           and I pad softly, breathe with Autumn
           through the hawk-wood on the hill.
           I am the shadow, the bite of the wind
        beneath the trees
           that run from hill to sea –

are gone. They have made my lands an
empty sky
                beneath the moon; my calls echo,
                unanswered.

The castle was found
unmapped and green-entangled on the hill in the rambles;
its walls, through crumbled, sang of kings
and heroes and swords and

the stone was rough and warm,
like granddad.

            I learnt my history on his knee
            and in childhood games of princes
            riding out from the fell-wood
            in the bright spear and glory of the morning.

And from those old walls I could see
sunlight, glancing off the sea
and away.

"you only like the idea of me..." by Alisa Lockwood

yes, I confess
I like the *idea* of you
I like this newfound faith.
I feel born again
into a world warmed by the sun of your hands;
where my skin is the pale evening sky
in which your fingertips leave galaxies of hidden stars.
I understand now the divinity
of a single breath,
of just one lost heartbeat
echoing against my palm.
life moves with an unbearable tenderness
every movement like a lingering caress –
your touch is shadow, light, wind, rain
eternal stillness and sudden storm
a fern unfurling slowly in the humid amazon
a trembling wet-winged butterfly
I find you everywhere and all around.

it is too easy to worship you.

but when you turn away
with eyes I don't recognise
as if to remind me
that I only serve your pleasure,
then I fear your vengeance
I fear that my flesh will be mute again,
that like the old volatile gods
you will make me cut out my heart,
in the knowledge that nothing is promised –
for even the greatest sacrifice
offers no certainties.

yet I believe in you
I must believe, because
in place of certainty
you give me, hope.

Rock, Scissors, Paper by Clare Scott

I sit chilled
stone deep still
on a
cold concrete   broken wood   rusty metal
park bench

until

cut
by a seagull's
sharp edged cries
slicing curves
in the sparkling sky

then

re-wrap myself
the cover encloses
to re-enter
the c h a o s

Carmarthen by Jeno Davies

First it was a Roman town a Roman legion army town

Then it was a Merlin town a castle and an oak tree town

Then it was a Tudor town a dead dog leaking sewage town

Then it was a Georgian town a big wig plump my pillow town

Then it was a Victorian town a toll gate and Rebecca town

Then it was a war town a joining up and dying town

Now it is a Tesco town a shop till you drop I want one town

The 2011 Winners
Judged by Sally Spedding

Horseshoe Bat by David J Costello

It must have been a keen blade
that eased you from night's heart.
God's own shrapnel
creasing the dark.
Your convulsing fragment
pressure-cracking the brittle black
like ice.

Transfixed beneath I watch
you stitch yourself
back to the sky.
An invisible repair
disappearing
as I acquire your blindness.
The whole world dissolving
around you.

You are the dark moon.
The nocturnal crescent
orbiting unseen.
The flung shape
that always returns.

The Carpenter's Daughter (Mary Anning) by Kathy Miles

(for Miriam: Saundersfoot 2010)

How could she resist?
The way the cliff parted its lips
to show bone, a tooth,
a skeleton peeping from the schist.

Her long skirts damp with the shuffle
and rush of small waves,
hair held back in its dark bonnet,
she scoured the shore for skulls and shells,
for a jaw or an eye socket,
the head of an ichthyosaur.

Occasionally she'd find a spine,
a crinoid coiled in clay,
pieces of vertebrae
prised gently from the cliff-face.
Her petticoats crusted with mud and sand,
hands raw from salt and cold.

Sometimes, distracted by the living,
she'd see a scuttling hermit-crag,
shrimps skip across a pool. And she'd imagine
them all dead, all frozen in stone,
and wondered, too, how she would look;
whether her wide skirts
would survive in blue lias,
and whether in two million years
her naked, indelicate bones
would be exposed by another's fossil hammer.

She hated days like this. Hot, humid,
sea mist caged by the sun, her boots
sweaty and stiff, and the water too calm,
like a solid karst of grief.
Days when flint yielded nothing
but its own glistening core,
no brittle star or belemnite, only grey heart.

So now when I see you
striding ahead of me on the shore,
head down, absorbed, your patchwork skirt
brushing the ridged sand,
black shoes ruined by salt,
pockets full of shells and pebbles,
quick eyes alert for ammonites,
I think of the carpenter's daughter
chipping out a living from the rocks,
searching for snakestones in the shale.
For those silent creatures sleeping
in their unforgiving cradles.

Night's Spy-glass by Moira Andrew

On the edge of silence, night
does her own thing, peers down
from a thousand quicksilver eyes,
finding us, snug as sardines,
in our wide double bed.

She can't be doing with our
lazy innocence, our looking-forward
to years of togetherness, snaps
imperious fingers, calls for
ever-stronger lenses, magnifies

a heart-problem here, a dodgy
knee there, pulling the rug
from under our complacency.
She shows her teeth, conjures
chaos music from overhead wires,

gives black-bud trees dancing
shoes, sits back and screws
a spy-glass into every star. She
sticks pins into each tender part,
Try this on for size, she says,

watching our every move
with clinical detachment. It
takes all our energy not to cry out,
simply to stroke the other's
skin and live until morning.

Judges' comments:

Horseshoe Bat, by David J Costello

'It must have been a keen blade
That eased you from night's heart...'

The exquisite precision of these opening lines perfectly conveys an almost surgical procedure, and while the poem's economy extends into a more mellow, introspective tone, I remained skewered to this small mammal's journey where there is no excess baggage, no self-indulgent clutter.

I hadn't heard of the Horseshoe bat, so I learnt something too. This is a magical and memorable work. A worthy winner.

The Carpenter's Daughter (Mary Anning), by Kathy Miles

'How could she resist?
The way the cliff parted its lips...'

The intriguing question at the start of this poem and the almost erotic image that follows, drew me deep into Mary Anning's obsessive world as she gathers fossils for a living. Each word, each assonance and phrase contrasts the dead world of 'those silent creatures sleeping in their unforgiving cradles' with that of a determined young girl born in 1799, who wonders if one day her own 'naked, indelicate bones' will too, become the same. The present-day ending reinforces the earlier sense of time past. Marvellous.

163

Night's Spy-glass, by Moira Andrew

'On the edge of silence, night
does her own thing...'

In this remarkable and disturbing poem, the all-seeing night, which,
without much thought on our part, accompanies most of us to bed, is
given a growing malevolence, playing on one of our worst fears -
will we still be alive in the morning? Here, she 'sits back and screws
a spay-glass into every star. She sticks a pin into each tender part...
watching every move...'
    I now check her out, unable to shake the following last two lines
from my mind, where the best we can do is 'simply to stroke the
other's skin and live until morning.'

Sally Spedding, July 2011

Specially Commended, 2011

Stitches by Fatima Al Matar

Giving birth to her
I was torn pieces of flesh
sewed together with nylon thread
between blood flooding and cord cutting
skin slipping away from skin
untidy cross stitches done with haste
new thresholds of pain and love mixing,
peaking, dancing a sloppy waltz.

It took a while before
two rivals of slit open skin
forgave and forgot,
integrated beautifully with nylon.

Five years later
sitting on the edge of the bed
last chore of the day
hands tired
I unpick stitches
pulling with my teeth
redundant binding
messy hemming done with haste
end of string refusing needle's eye
making her school skirt fit.

baby growing out of her clothes,
mother ageing

another stitch undone
another knot released.

Ah, you should see the mighty Deere by Mary Ryan

Ah, you should see the mighty Deere roll by,
big as a house; the true Colossus
of the country lane.
There's a lad up there somewhere,
high in his eyrie, riding his war horse
to battle, with its heraldry of clean green
and the acid yellow of tired buttercups,
invincible on cruise control.
He is tethered by his phone and iPod
to a talking world, the soil a long way down.
the machine is in charge now,
its tread widening without mercy,
roots of twisted beech rent in its wake.
Unheard, the any old bird sings a lone lament
for days when yards had hens
and a baby Dexta hiccupped slowly up the lane.

In Bloom by Tom Gatehouse

You will leave the days of open skies,

blushing sunsets and wooden pub benches,

on balmy evenings in June and July,

    To the city,

        Where there is always a lift, or an escalator,

            or a staircase in the penumbra.

        Where the days pass, ascending, descending,

    chasing a living. So you only come out at night,

amidst the ashtrays, glasses, guitars and

other musical instruments

you cannot name.

You leave the house with wine in your belly

    and a spring in your step, there is nothing to fear,

        nothing to fear in the doorways that reek like
phone boxes.

You seek one who awaits or eludes you,

but later on it's always the same,

holding onto the bar for dear life

as she mixes another drink you don't need.

It's these late amities

made and unmade in murky hours

[and with people whose names
escape you]

but they saw you,
and you them.

You learn fast:

taxi ranks, routes, night buses,

the going price of green on the street,

How to wash in filthy closets where the water runs cold,

how to grope for light switches in dark corridors

in which dirt and dust stick to the soles of
your feet.
Your walls will rot, your pipes will burst,

as preposterous speed your blinds crunch down, then up
again,

your footsteps will echo along vacant

platforms,

tapping out the seconds 'til

the next

train.

so much best remembered

that escapes you

so much best forgotten

that doesn't.

Perce Blackborow by Glyn Edwards
(Shackleton's 26th crew member)

By following the cat to the cradling shadows
the Captain had found me in the hull
rolling the ship's pet to sleep, folding its ears.

He kept his stowaways, fed us routine, purpose:
We were dripping echoes of his youth.

The Endeavour smacked the water
for months and I filled a shivery diary
about the cold and the hounds and the quiet men.

I studies how the position of the sun
spoils photographs, scorns navigation. How it lights
thoughts of grey chapels in slate valleys.

Others hated leaving the ship that night,
couldn't watch their home snap and sink below packed ice
but I was soothed by our lonely landscape.

We fought nature's silences with stories, filled empty
spaces with football pitches and terraces of tents.
Some waited to be found, I explored

New whites that bordered the emptiness,
discovered how to stew a dog, feed it
to another. Savoured hanging heavy clothes

in the hopeful chill. Learnt how to hide
my limp from the surgeon's suspicions
by stepping forward first. Always.

Before the panic of flagwavers and photographers
at the quay I shuffled numbly
from the rescue ship. Desperate not to reveal

how much I'd given to the snow. But, in the stark room
the Boss led me to, he made me sit and unwrap
my boots. I surrendered the raw black joints.

He knew the feet would be parted from me,
but that I would not drift from the sea.

I lean on the balustrade each morning,
watch orange seep from the sky
and hear wild noises carried on water.

Lightwells by Alana Kelsall

Put the sky there   in the middle

don't think about how cramped it looks

between the iced-up walls and the tree

on the corner   or what a father might think

about the five decades he had in him

when he left   think about how things

might begin if the footpaths had been banked up

with snow   beds and desks to be assembled

with cold-knuckled fingers   a local just a street away

where most nights a father might talk about his son

a goalkeeper on the other side of the world

and the father's early morning calls across the Pacific

loosening the cords of work and home

then the long wait for the plane to touch down

now turn one desk to face a northerly window

this is the February sky that fills and

fills with clouds   don't think about endings

or where the shared space stops

up here the cloths dry on the landing

the air is thick with the smell of sliced onions

and that bang is the sound of the wok

on the metal plate as the rather worries

the sauce around the curry with a flick of his wrist

leave the door open   there's hope

in every room the son sits in

the father's up at dawn to trawl for house

for messages   he counts the months left

till the next season   a new rasp in his voice

when he argues with his son about

the best strategy or wakes up on the couch

to his phone ringing   another dead end

listen to the creak on the stairs

the son takes them   two at a time

to grab his sat-nav   he's surprised

at the fluttering of his parents' thoughts

thinks of his sureness of touch on the field

and that spot at the top of the hill

where his car jumps forward and lifts

and how each day is just like that

up here the sky fits anywhere

the son packs his bag with gloves and shorts

his hands folding over each other like leaves

he calls up the stairs   *See ya Mum*

the front door sucking the sound out

later from the kitchen below

the clatter of dishes in the small square of ink

the father busying himself while he waits for news

both of them listening for the sounds

of the other rooms they have yet to grow into

The Kasaks of Mongolia by Mary Irvine

The Kasaks of Mongolia
do not name their horses
yet have six hundred words
for the colour of horses

Once I was on a horse
not riding
staying on
the boy leading the horse
was called maladjusted
here
I was maladjusted

All the children are labelled
the evacuees on the platform
the children in their special schools

Sometimes the labels get confused
and the children lose their identity

The Kasaks think more of their horses

Belted Gabardines by Joy Winkler

Washday afternoons are for walking:
away from the swelter of shrinking rooms,
heated quarrelling. Away from the grip
of the steel shouldered mangle, wet walls,
sweat of Sunday left-overs.

Away from the red temper she kneads
into the pulp of her backache with a swollen
wedding-banded fist, while a hissing
July fire slaps our cheeks, stamps
crimson circles onto our pastry skin.

Washday afternoons are for banking up
embers with damp coal, locking them
behind a screen of stiff-armed shirts,
half dry overalls. They are for outdoor
shoes, for outdoor best behaviour.

We hold hands, buttoned together, hooded
against summer mizzle. We are school- minded
crossing the road like odd coloured sheep.
In our belted gabardines we are different people.
We stand at the five-barred gate, throw old bread

to peck-quick hens as weak sunshine colours them
russet on brown. She laughs and emerald seeps back
into field edges, she tells us stories and grey
clouds are buffeted away by a menagerie of white.
In our belted Gabardines we are in a picture book

Aim by Louise Wilford

strange how it comes to this, the distant black astonished mouths
settling in a steady row, ready to spit oblivion.

> Elizabeth standing by the upright

piano,

> cock-eyed red cross

the grass is trampled here, mud leak through weedy fronds,
the dance-floor for a score of twitching men. St Vitas. Cirspin
Crispianus

> the high pink smell of moor-top

heather

> giant blades of granite
> curlew's siren hoot.

in a split slice of a second, I glimpse a kestrel, black scratch in the
half-cooked sky, breathing a tower of air, dropping

> Elizabeth.
> black eye-lash on her white cheek

strange how I'll never touch

Who will tell her? A blank white hand with a telegram
afraid to say I shop like marionette my bowels burned

they'll have to scrub the stench off the khaki later
when they cart what's left off my tongue pressing my palate my
teeth
chattering my arms jerking as the clicks like children's
claps like nails on teeth dog's claws on pavements belt buckles

180

harness rings

the kestrel drops
in a cloudless yellow dawn

through the scent of heather

Seal Clubbing by Glyn Edwards
(Bardsey Island)

it is dusk when they come
onto the clumsy cold sand
like liquid rocks.

Soon there will be no light
on the Blesses Isle to judge
whether starvation was reason enough.

I feel the fracture from hiding inside,
caged by sunless storms
and crying winds. Bruised

fuchsia burst open again
oystercatchers creak as playground swings,
endless sky a puffinbeak of indecision
but there was nobody in the silent lighthouse,
peeling farmhouse or voiceless abbey
to make the thunder of hunger relent
or slip this fence post from my hand.

In six weeks, dolphin will crest the Sound
and pilgrims step wearily
from rested motorboats.

Quiet men will kick bladderwrack
from the harbour's slope
mermaids could haunt.

I will mend lobsterpots with withies
and eave my confession
back into the waves.

Girl on the underground by Alisa Lockwood

The way your bitten thumb
casually taps through music tracks,
'cool age' etched on your sandal strap
tie-dyed peace sign stretched over your belly
youth's banal symbolism
so very normal and ordinary

No makeup, just a wrist-flick of onyx
darkening the fragile ends of downcast lashes
you yawn haphazardly, like a half-grown animal
small nostrils widening

But somehow the top of your head
the not quite straight parting
announces a sinister innocence
dishevelled shadow of a hand pushing back

Translucent, almost invisible
paper-thin, you mush have caught fire easily
edges of burnt flesh curled up
under the glowing tip
the pale glint of his fingerprint
winks at me from your forearm
among the lines you drew
blood to erase his touch,
to reclaim your pain

Before I can look away
the void in your eyes terrifying blue
hits me like a breached sound barrier

Bridgend by Mark Lock

Friends.
Friends of friends.
Mutual friends.

Friends that will choke up your Twitter account.
Bebo and Facebook – the modern self-doubt.
Mobile phone'd girls in their barely there tops.
Boys without shirts, all reversed mirror shots.
The back bone is virtual.
The street corner gone.

The sickly stale air of the season end fair,
The town that will slowly fall down round your ears.
Injecting Dianabol, Androlic, Testolic.
The Thursday and Friday night bursts of euphoric.
All flat, dead and still in the
Pale of the morning.

Did you peer down the tunnel of years with no hope?
A life of uncertainty – desperate and cold.
A shift up the road to a colder abode.
A job with no end, clothes smelling of smoke.
Sitting alone in the
Years that you broke.

The park where you ran and you played as a child
Where you'd hang out and spin and you'd jump and you'd slide.
Now you hang and you slide, slipping straight out of life.
A fading young light in a soft winter night.
(The birds cease their noise
As their bright eyes shut tight)

When the tabloids grew bored and they sucked themselves shut,
And the London press left with a critical tut,
The spaces you left still all needed filling
Your friends and your family still feel like they're falling
Your friends and your family
Are never forgetting.

Mutual friends.
Friends of friends.
Friends.

Silas Jones by Anthony Fisher

He was a small man, belted gabardine raincoat
and thirteen languages tucked around his person.
A fine hand disciplined: copper plate, italic,
sharp steel nib, dipped in iron blue ink,
smooth, white paper that crackled when folded.
Even in an unknown tongue it could be enjoyed
each word soaking in to the hand that stroked it..

One grey day I looked for Silas Jones
but all I found was a mist of languages
drifting in the Welsh air.

Ode to Joy by Emily Hinshelwood

Freude, schooner Gotterfunken,
Tochter aus Elysium
      Joy, beautiful spark of Gods
      Daughter of Elysium

It was the first record we ever bought her.
We used to blast it out and all dance round
the kitchen conducting the chorus. The cat
well-scarpered, the plates rattling on the gas stove.

Now in the Festival Hall the choir is pounding it out.
She is at the back, her round face just reaching
over the rows of altos – like the sun on the horizon.
She is so much shorter than she was – and shrinking.

Reminds me that the sun has to set
and will sink below the sea
and will take away all the light and warmth
that we've enjoyed the whole day long.

Beacon and Elks by Sheila Barksdale

This breezy hilltop whose rumoured excitement was
Vikings chewing up the locals, has lovely views
and a gale off the ocean which cuts like a knife.
There's the Vicar straying off his patch,
headed for the car-park maybe; God bless his Thermos.
I'm all for early elevenses myself, having skipped breakfast.
"Alle goode loppyns I plunge and I drenche"-
I'll try that one on him, he's a history man,
tells me not all history is hogwash, it's just that
the calendar is a kind of thrifty butcher
turning the discordant centuries
into a tidy string of sausages.

Lovely views all round: nothing else up here,
the ground's as heavy as soggy toast.
Bleep bleep (that's my metal detector) and hey –
a squashed helmet from the Bronze Age! Nice!
Was it reindeer or was it moose
that they worshipped back then?
Because look, see this rusty metal thing –
er- for a moment, I really thought…
just the broken handle of an incredibly large
frying pan big enough to fry a reindeer in, or an elk:
probably those nuisance campers from two summers ago.

Hah! A fork!
Hmm, stainless steel. Pity, could have been a Roman brooch.
they say forks were a fancy thing come over from the Continent.
Imagine being the one who first sighted the Armada: holy smoke!
I suppose I'd better go and chat to the old boy;
last time we chatted over a pint a the Miners Arms,
I told him, "It's history that sizzles,

all the world religions are like shrunken mushrooms
sculling around a slowly congealing sea
of indifference."
He laughed and said, "You're no pagan:
you have dangerous opinions."

Mackworth Street by Jenny Powell

In his boy of six memories
there is only the backyard,
the rest is what they told him,

the terraced house, bricks
slotted in close and tight
along the row, down to the corner.

A close shave between each house,
arguments domino toppling
until you would swear

they were all at it, the whole
bloody lot of them and everyone's
kids sent outside to play.

The brick brown gloom settling
through the street like a valley
fog and Uncle Charlie's dead

in the mine. Who's next? Who's
next? 60 years after the better life
he's back. In his travel log

the event is recorded;
28 Mackworth Street.
Nobody home.

The Painter's Holiday by Jenny Powell

His last holiday at Scarborough,
bucket and spade, his mother's

hand. High cliffs with jagged lines
descending into sea, streams

of light stabbing the crests
of swell, weakening sun a pale

lemon across their track,
the wind's gasp, sharp and crisp.

At the cottage he painted
his mother's legs purple blue

and swollen. He painted her
out by the door, hollyhocks

sharing the same hue.
Her legs, balloons of lead

that would leave her earth
bound, dust to dust. When

he was six she was dead.
Seasons turned to the shiver

of sleeting rain, the light
lined with shadows.

Don't call your father a bastard by Ceri Rees

Don't call your father a bastard,
especially seeing as how,
the man you call Dad ain't your father.
So who's the bastard now?

Index of titles

A pen portrait of my ex-lover by Penny James	135
A walk with God by Patricia Bellotti	107
A weekend at the coast by Meghan Tally	150
Ah, you should see the mighty Deere by Mary Ryan	168
Aim by Louise Wilford	180
Bags by Roger Barnett	31
Balancing Mixed Vegetables On A Motorway Bridge by Clive Gilson	23
Barry Island revisited by Emyr Jones	63
Beacon and Elks by Sheila Barksdale	188
Belted Gaberdines by Joy Winkler	179
Birthday Lunch by Pip Smith	76
Boireann by Graham Burchell	64
Bridgend by Mark Lock	184
Bus Ride by Josiah Rowlands	37
Buzzards over Fleam Dyke by Harry Goode	104
Carmarthen by Jeno Davies	156
Concrete by Gavin Price	7
Connecting by Leah Armstead	34
Corposant by Gareth Roberts	95
Cynical Saviour? (maybe) by John Lusardi	144
Different by Jo Walters	146
Don't call your father a bastard by Ceri Rees	192
Easter Monday by Isobel Norris	108
Estuary by Gareth Roberts	151
Extinction by Cerys Jones	35
Finding the Darkness by James Knox Whittet	111
First Baron Cawdor of Castlemartin by Emily Hinshelwood	110
Flies on Coke by Ellie Madden	69
Flights of Fancy by Richard Garman	21
Forget-Me-Not by Leah Ebdon	56
Fragments of Cardiff by Kate Scarratt	24
Girl on the Underground by Alisa Lockwood	183
Going Back by Terry Jones	147

Head Case by Phil Knight   114

Her hairs not short by Gavin Price   17

Hide by Jane Galletly   57

His greatest fear by Leah Armstead   78

Horseshoe Bat by David J Costello   159

I don't do hugs by Eloise Williams   45

In 1968... by John Gallas   22

In Bloom by Tom Gatehouse   169

Inside Out by Anthony Keating   33

Izzy by Nigel Ormond   123

Jetsam by Noel Williams   133

Kasaks of Mongolia by Mary Irvine   178

Learning from Buzzards by Roger Elkin   58

lights in water by John Gallas   113

Lightwells by Alana Kelsall   174

Litzmannstadt 1941 by Sally Spedding   121

Llandudno by Helen Johnson   142

Luna by Ben Ziman-Bright   101

Mackworth Street by Jenny Powell   190

Mad Mike: he's a motorbike manual
by (Merv Read)/Read the Rock Poet   73

Mr Selvridge Sketches by Richard Halperin   140

My Body is Old Porridge by Eloise Williams   9

Nan Follows the Bikers on a Day Out by Eluned Rees   85

Night's Spy-glass by Moira Andrew   162

Ode to Joy by Emily Hinshelwood   187

on Davaar Island by John Gallas   71

On deck with Alun Lewis, the secret sleeper
by Owen Lowery   53

On Eric Gill - typophile etc. by Emily Hinshelwood   26

One more to work the Oliver Hammer 1899
by Silvia Millward   105

Pen-y-Fan Revisited by Christopher Rogers   61

Perce Blackbarrow by Glyn Edwards   172

Pins by Graham Burchell   102
Polly by Ashley Bovan   134
Polyfiller by Clare Ferguson-Walker   43
Rails by Lynn Roberts   87
Rock, Scissors, Paper by Clare Scott   155
Seal Clubbing by Glyn Edwards   182
Shifts by Pat Borthwick   137
Shipbuilding by David Ford   93
Show me the money by Amanda Weeks   66
Silas Jones by Anthony Fisher   186
Solar Plexus by Jane Fox   19
space by Amanda Weeks   11
Still by Sue Lovell   138
Stitches by Fatima Al Matar   167
Swansea Bay Promenade by Isobel Norris   30
the 2154 of this land by Steve Garside   149
The Carpenter's Daughter by Kathy Miles   160
The day I ate what I thought was a magic mushroom
   by Leah Armstead   116
The Gatekeeper by Deborah Harvey   109
The Milky Way by Megan Vaughan   79
the origami lesson by John Gallas   83
The Painter's Holiday by Jenny Powell   191
The Size Zero Debate by Emma Sullivan   36
To Orpheus@lyre.com by Kate Noakes   28
Tower by John Watkins   75
Trout by James Gower   55
Union Cat by Patricia Bellotti   68
Urban Tales by Phil Knight   29
Visually-speaking by Emily Hinshelwood   41
Waiting by Jane Fox   125
Wasp... by David Butler   99
Wasted by Gareth Roberts   97
Watching Layers Form by Jenny Adamthwaite   60

What I am by Carrie-Ann Fry   32
When she was very young by Rebecca Carrington   98
When you know the party's over... by J.S. Watts   143
"you only like the idea of me..." by Alisa Lockwood   153

Printed in Great Britain
by Amazon